"How Does SHE Manage?"

Four Very Different Women
Swap Ideas on Managing a
Home and Family...

"How Does SHE Manage?"

Sarah   Chani   Dena   Tova

Yael Wiesner

FELDHEIM PUBLISHERS
JERUSALEM   NEW YORK

FELDHEIM PUBLISHERS
POB 43163/ Jerusalem, Israel
208 Airport Executive Park
Nanuet, NY 10954

www.feldheim.com

10 9 8 7 6 5 4 3 2 1

Printed in Israel

*To my very special
husband and children —
it's a privilege and a pleasure
to manage our home!*

Acknowledgments

FIRST AND FOREMOST, I would like to use this opportunity to thank Hashem for all He has given me and all that He continues to bestow upon me in His infinite kindness. Specifically, I thank Him for the growth I have experienced in managing my own home and for the clear *siyata diShmaya* that led to the publishing of this book.

Thank you to the original Resource Group — official and unofficial members — Sharon Broder, Estie Cooper, Miriam Dvorin, Bassi Gruen, Leora Gruen, Leah Hass, Avigayil Hittman, Shprintze Ingber, Dvorah Lerner, Michelle Lerner, Avigayil Levin, Shulamis Liebenstien, Yael Mermelstein, Abigail Neckameyer, Pnina Neiman, Mimi Novak, Dalia Ratner, Karen Thaler, Esther Weissman and Becky Willig. This book is the fruit of your ideas. Our group has changed my life and will now *b'ezras Hashem* help others. Thank you and *yasher ko'ach* to each of you!

I am especially grateful to Miriam Dvorin. Thank you for your professional and creative advice.

A special thank you to Yael Mermelstein. Aside from your insightful Resource Group tips, I am grateful for your professional advice, your review of this book and, above all, our everlasting friendship.

I am indebted to Bassi Gruen for the birth of this book, labor pains and all. Your assistance in its initial stages was crucial in preparing it for publication, and your review and afterword are invaluable to me.

Thank you Esther Heller for your professional advice.

Thank you to Aidel Teller and Tamar Ansh for your gracious reviews of the book.

I am so grateful to my neighbor, Libby Roberts. Your dedication to this project around the clock cannot be repaid. I simply could not have managed without you!

Thank you Rebbetzin Yehudis Salenger. Attending your *chinuch ha-banim* classes for over a decade has molded my attitudes toward my children and my life, as well as those of many of the members of our Resource Group. Each of us has incorporated your insightful lessons into our own parenting — each in her own way — and these different ideas repeatedly came up in our meetings. If any of the *chinuch* lessons you have taught us have been misrepresented in this book, I take full responsibility. May you continue to have much *siyata diShmaya* in your great work.

Thank you Rebbetzin Frumma Altusky, Rebbetzin Yitty Neustadt, Rebbetzin Miriam Freilich and Rebbetzin Gila Levitt, whose words of *chizuk* have made lasting impressions on my life and in the building of my home. Echoes of your advice come through in this book as well.

Thank you Vivi Keilson for bringing Sarah, Tova, Chani and Dena to life. Your talent and creativity are evident in all of your illustrations. It was a pleasure to work with you!

Thank you Sherie Gross for your excellent editing. Your eye for consistency and talent with language brought the book to its final success. Thank you Anita Steinberg for your lovely design, Michael Silverstein for your fabulous cover design, Eden Chachamtzedek for your meticulous typesetting work, and to the entire Feldheim staff. I appreciate all your input and energy in publishing this book.

Thank you Ilana Spierer, Miriam Wolf and Yehudis Margolis, my special cousins, for your input.

Thank you Dr. Dov and Debbie Rosen, Rabbi Yehuda and Rivki Werblowsky and Rabbi Yisrael Chaim and Orly Cohen, my siblings and siblings-in-law, for being constant positive forces in my life. May we continue sharing *simchahs* together.

Thank you to my parents, Mr. Vel and Naomi Werblowsky, for the hours spent typing and editing my book! It is another classic example of your dedication to your children. Thank you for all that you've given us and continue to give us. May Hashem grant you many years of happiness, good health and *nachas* from all your children and grandchildren.

Thank you to my in-laws, Mr. Joseph and Jacqueline Wiesner, for constantly standing by our side. Your presence in our home has sweetened up our lives in more ways than one. May Hashem grant you good health, happiness and *nachas* from all of us, always.

To my big girls — thank you for being my right hands!

To all of my children — your shining faces give me strength! Thank you for the tremendous *nachas* you give us. May you continue to grow in your *avodas Hashem* in good health and happiness, always.

My greatest *hakaras ha-tov* goes to my husband, who knows the real secret to "How does SHE manage?" It is my greatest *zechus* to manage our home. May Hashem continue to help us all grow in Torah and *yiras Shamayim* and grant us *berachah ve'hatzlachah* as we continue building our fortress.

Contents

Introduction .... *xiii*

Let's Meet the Women in Our Resource Group .... *xix*

Autumn — Elul, Tishrei, Cheshvan

Chapter 1:   Morning Routines *1*

Chapter 2:   Evening Routines *9*

Chapter 3:   Preparing for the Yamim Nora'im *21*

Chapter 4:   Maintaining Daily Ruchnius *33*

Winter — Kislev, Teves, Shevat

Chapter 5:   Shabbos *47*

Chapter 6:   Menu Planning *61*

Chapter 7:   Making Laundry Manageable *83*

Chapter 8:   Bored Children *93*

Spring — Adar, Nisan, Iyar

Chapter 9:   Organizing the Home – I *107*

Chapter 10:   Organizing the Home – II *125*

Chapter 11:   Cleaning and Home Maintenance *137*

Chapter 12:   Pesach *163*

Summer — Sivan, Tamuz, Av

Chapter 13:   Recharging *181*

Chapter 14:   Family Vacation *189*

Chapter 15:   Prioritizing *199*

Afterword: Start Your Own Resource Group *213*

Index of Checklists, Tips and Ideas

Dinner Ideas, *78*

Examples of Age Appropriate Jobs, *161*

General Organization Tips, *134*

Money Management Tips, *81*

No-fuss Food and Snacks for the Month of Nisan, *177*

Packing Lists, *196*

Paper Projects, *102*

Pesach Activities for Ages 5–8, *174*

Pesach Job Suggestions between Purim and
   Rosh Chodesh Nisan, *166*

Popular Activities in Tova's House, *100*

Sandwich and Lunch Ideas, *73*

Self-Analysis Questions, *206*

Shabbos Checklist, *60*

Stain Removal Tips, *91*

Ten Step System for Delegating
   Housework to Children, *159*

Ten Steps to Declutter Your House, *133*

What to Clean, *157*

Introduction

How This Book Was Born

I REMEMBER THE FIRST home management book I read. It was about fifteen years ago, a few months after the birth of my first child. At the time, I was working at a high-pressured job. Having grown up in a time and environment in which it was unnecessary for children to have added responsibilities of their own, I was unprepared for my daily challenges. Caring for a baby, keeping a clean and organized home, managing a demanding job, and still finding time and energy to prepare wholesome dinners for my husband and myself was more than I could handle. I recognized that I needed help, so I borrowed a book from a friend.

I read a few chapters and bemoaned my fate: Would I ever be a *balabusta*? According to the book, a qualified homemaker's pots are polished with steel wool after every use so that they don't look tarnished. Food in polished pots is far more appetizing, after all. A proper homemaker quickly organizes a different section of the closet or cupboards every day. When her husband returns from his day out of the house, Mrs. Balabusta has a steaming hot dinner on the table for him — complete with soup, salad and dessert. The baby has already been fed and is now gurgling happily in his playpen. The baby's knees and hands stay clean while he is crawling because his efficient mother washes the floor often. Maybe I read too many chapters in succession, but all I could do was cry.

On second thought, I was angry. The author may have been

right, I supposed, but she didn't understand me. Didn't she know my baby kept me up every night? Didn't she know I cooked my very first pot of noodles the week after *sheva berachos* and even succeeded in ruining a loaf of prepared gefilte fish? Didn't she know that a dishwasher washes the dishes, a cleaning lady cleans the house, and potato kugels are bought at the takeout store? Why was she suggesting that I had to do it all? And to perfection, at that! Needless to say, the book didn't help me much, so I turned to my friends and mentors for tips and advice.

As my family grew, tidbits from friends weren't sufficient. I had a few different walking partners over the years and I would pick their brains for almost a full hour on all topics — laundry methods, evening routines, knowledge of nutrition and easy recipes — you name it! I ran much of my home based on what I learned from those walks.

One day, I got a phone call from a good friend. "I'm drowning in laundry," she admitted. "I barely do it, hate folding it and almost never put it away. You have to help me." By then, I had mastered my own laundry routine. I helped her discover the root of her problem and gave her some tips and *chizuk*. I have another friend who is constantly asking me for advice on technical success around the house. In return, she came over and helped me rearrange things to make my kitchen more functional.

After one of our conversations, the proverbial light bulb popped up over my head. If anyone had been in the room, they would have seen it. My friends and I had all picked up so many tricks and shortcuts over the years as we tried to figure out homemaking, and yet we all had a long way to go. But now I was certain that I had discovered the comprehensive answer to perfect our skills and schedules: We would share all our learned wisdom with each other in an organized way. Exchanging tidbits during morning walks wasn't enough; we would have "scheduled sharing!" After all, even I had finally figured out how to run a home smoothly with a husband in *kollel* and three energetic children... except that by now, I had six. Whatever I had deciphered already needed a complete overhaul because of my family's ever-growing needs.

Inspired, I called a few good friends who I thought might be interested and mapped out my brainstorm idea with them: a bimonthly "Resource Group" with all my friends in my living room. Everyone was excited to give it a try. We had about ten to fifteen women in our group, ranging in age from their early to late thirties. Each session focused on crucial home management topics: decluttering, menu planning, recharging oneself, preparing for Yom Tov, entertaining children, etc. At every meeting, one of us would present a twenty minute talk on the subject. She would explain her precise method and helpful tips for tackling that area of homemaking. It was eye-opening to discover that each woman shone in certain areas and was weak in others — to my delight, this was normal! After the main speaker, each member of the group had a turn to speak for a few minutes; she either offered her best tricks on the topic or asked for everyone's advice.

We all looked forward to the Resource Group. We considered gathering every week, but in order for the idea to succeed, there had to be enough time between sessions to absorb the information and apply it. Every meeting gave us realistic, applicable ideas for our homes, our families and ourselves. The beauty of it all was that the ideas came from different people with different personalities. Nobody claimed to be an expert on any topic. It was much easier to accept that way, or to disregard if it didn't fit with our personalities. The running theme in our Resource Group was clear — there is no one rule or one way to run a successful home. We all shared the same common goal — to be productive, efficient and happy home-makers — yet we all achieved it differently. Many of us felt that we had uncovered a treasure. A friend and member of the Resource Group, Bassi Gruen, wrote an article about it in *Mishpacha* maga-zine: "*A Virtual Goldmine as Close as Your Neighbor's Living Room.*" The article received a lot of positive feedback. In the three years the Resource Groups met in my home, we exhausted every topic. In fact, we discussed most topics twice, squeezing every last drop of information out of all of us. My notebook was stuffed and my home was flourishing.

Sitting on my neighbor's couch one day, I flipped through a home management book that was lying around. It was written by a different author than the first book that I had read, but this book, too, contained a wealth of information that could be ap-preciated by only one personality type: "the perfect homemaker." This time I was confident in my homemaking skills, and reading the book didn't anger me, but I found myself disagreeing with the author's attitude and approach. I wished I could help all the women who picked up this book searching for help and *chizuk*, only to be discouraged by its one-dimensional nature.

I decided to compile all the information the Resource Group had given me over the years. I wrote it as a dialogue that rec-reates the group sessions, so that all types of women could feel connected to the ideas, without feeling intimidated by them. After reviewing my notes, I noticed that though there were more than fifteen women involved, most of the advice offered could be divided into one of four different categories of women: the ex-tremely organized woman, the well-balanced woman, the mini-mum-fuss woman, and the working woman. In truth, although we all lean towards one of these categories, every woman has all four of these personalities within her, depending on her stage in life or the area of the home she is tending to.

In structuring this book, I organized the methods and tips that we shared in our meetings by attributing them to these four defined personalities. It is important to note that in the actual sessions, no one person gave all the tips that fit her personality type.

How to Use This Book

This book should not be read in one sitting. You might be tempted to read it from cover to cover so that you can fix everything that needs to be fixed tomorrow. Please don't do that! Some tips and methods take more preplanning and rearranging than others. The chapters are arranged according to the Hebrew calendar year, and include the things that are logical to work on in each season.

As you read, you can use a highlighter or a pencil to mark off which systems or ideas will work best for you. Since every person has their own unique style and needs, some of the information in this book will appeal to you, and some will not. You don't need to implement every suggestion in order to feel like a *balabusta*! (Though reading them can help you understand your friends, mother, and mother-in-law better!)

It is worthwhile to reread the suggestions in the book every so often, as we are constantly growing and graduating to the next level of success in home management. What may seem daunting to you this year, may be manageable in a year or two down the line. You might also find that after you've already implemented some ideas, you'll be equipped to handle more.

This book is set up as a conversation between four friends, which lends itself to relaxed reading. It would have been ideal to include tips from all four personalities in each chapter, but it wouldn't have been true to life. A highly organized individual will naturally have the most tips on home organization and cleanliness. A successful working mother, by definition, is exceptional at prioritizing schedules and discovering shortcuts. Each woman naturally has certain areas of expertise about which she feels most competent to share, yet also has tidbits and valuable suggestions for other topics. The four women and their accompanying caricatures will help you identify yourself as well as others in your life. Find the one you best relate to, and start implementing the ideas that appeal to you!

For quick and easy reference, I have included highlights of the ideas as shoulder captions, as well as a variety of lists which include many handy suggestions.

It is my sincere hope that this book be a *shaliach ne'eman*, a faithful messenger, to help all Jewish women. To all you "naturals" out there, I hope the advice and methods serve to help you sharpen your homemaking techniques. To those of us whose home management doesn't come so easily and who need this book most, I hope that you'll find many practical resources in this book and — just as important — the empathetic voices of women like yourselves.

May Hashem derive *nachas* from us all and give each one of us continued *siyata diShmaya* in building a *bayis ne'eman b'Yisrael*.

Let's Meet the Women in
Our Resource Group

Sarah

**EXTREMELY ORGANIZED AND
FOCUSED ON CLEANLINESS**

My motto is, "A place for everything and everything in its place." Cleaning and organizing come naturally to me. I am also very scheduled and focused. Because I am so organized, I can find time in my life for many extras. The serene environment I have created in my home allows my family to grow and flourish. You'll hear a lot of my fantastic ideas in areas such as home organizing, cleaning and preparing for Shabbos and Pesach.

To me, "managing" means preparing well-balanced meals, having a clean and organized home, clean clothes and a happy family, complete with spiritual growth. I manage 90% of the time—at least.

Tova

WELL-BALANCED AND SOMEWHAT LAID-BACK

My motto is, "A home should be clean enough to be healthy but messy enough to be happy." I have a well-balanced approach toward managing my life, and I am full of *simchas ha-chaim*, joy of living. I am quite successful at running a functional, productive home, although sometimes I'm laid-back when it comes to housework. I enjoy implementing the tips I have learned at the Resource Group as long as they apply to my nature. You will like what I have to say on topics such as child-rearing, nurturing yourself, maintaining your *ruchnius* on a daily basis and some of my other "out of the box" ideas.

To me, "managing" means being as productive and efficient as possible without letting the tension of achieving proper maintenance ruin my ultimate goal: creating a pleasant, warm environment for my family.

Chani

MINIMUM FUSS AND CREATIVE

My motto is, "As long as I can find the floor, we're okay." I don't see a value in constantly cleaning my home. Most of the time, I don't notice the mess and I function reasonably well despite it. When my friends discuss the time they spend on cleaning and organizing their homes, I find it hard to relate. The meals I prepare are simple, yet healthy. The ideas and tips I have on all topics are uncomplicated and practical — even comical at times! I appreciate the Resource Group because it has given me key tips on how to improve the functioning of my home without forcing me to commit to a whole program of organization.

To me, "managing" means the ability to serve cornflakes for dinner while keeping a smile on my face and exhibiting proper *middos* around my family.

Dena

WORKING WOMAN

My motto is, "How can I squeeze thirty hours into twenty-four?" Everything must run smoothly in my house because I am not around enough hours in the day to pick up the slack. Though my ideals and priorities are extremely thought out, I still appreciate many of the tips offered at the Resource Group, and I am very good at choosing the ones that work best in light of my busy schedule. Expressing myself outside the home gives me the inner strength and fuel to manage my home properly. You'll discover from my tips that even though I have no spare time, I try to "do it all."

To me, "managing" means succeeding in my role as a wife, mother and homemaker while making a positive contribution outside the home as well.

Autumn —
Elul, Tishrei, Cheshvan

Chapter 1

Morning Routines

Sending the Family Off Cheerfully and Efficiently

Tova: I'm a bit rusty after an entire summer vacation when almost every day feels like a lazy Sunday morning. Come September 1st and it's hard to go straight into the "Everybody up; don't be late" mode. My morning routine needs a little tune-up. Can we get some ideas on how to run a successful morning?

Transitioning from vacation to school

Dena: I can almost say that I have a "degree" in efficient morning routines! I must be super organized in getting the kids out on time, because I can't be late for work. After vacation, I ease my children into the early morning routine starting a few days before school begins, since they can't go cold turkey from vacation mode to school schedule. They got used to these practice runs every year and they humor me.

Preparing the night before

The secret to success in the morning is preparing the night before. I'm sure that most of what I'm about to tell you is not new — it's just that we don't always do it.

Part of our bedtime routine is picking out the kids' clothing with them and locating their shoes. I have some very finicky children and this takes time. I even do this with the older children, making sure that their clothes are clean and ironed the way they like them. I don't have time in the morning for temper tantrums that could have easily been prevented.

Every evening, I make sure that the children pack up their book bags with all the books and items they need for the next day (permission slips, money, gym clothes, etc.). I begin ingraining these good habits in my children when they start first grade. It teaches them to be responsible and on time. I also prepare my own work bag and the baby's bag the night before so that I'll have more time in the morning to give the children the attention that they need.

No matter how tired I am, it's worth it for me to take twenty minutes in the evening to prepare all the sandwiches and snacks for the next day. I even set the breakfast table with the dairy tablecloth, bowls, spoons and cereal for the early risers. I always use paper goods for breakfast since I don't have time to do the breakfast dishes. My kids eat as soon as they wake up. I find that eating right away gives them the strength to deal with the morning better.

Tova: You really are organized! Does your husband help you?

Dena: He is very happy to help, but honestly, we found that doing morning routine together just didn't work well. We sort of just got in each other's way, and wound up doubling each other's efforts. Like, we'd both prepare clothes for the kids, or we'd both wash our toddler's hands *negel vasser*! Truth is, I don't mind the morning rush; I'm really focused in the morning and work well under pressure.

Husband's help

Tova: How do you keep your kids calm and happy when you feel so pressured yourself to get going?

Music and treats

Dena: I play music while we're getting ready. Some nice children's CDs with a morning theme add a lot to the atmosphere. I also periodically give the children a special prize or treat if they've stuck to the schedule and made sure to be ready on time. I make sure to keep the prizes enticing so that they stay motivated. Don't get me wrong — I can regale you with many a story about a terrible morning; we all have them. But these are my best tips, and they work for most of the time.

Sarah: Dena, you've covered almost everything! I just have a few of my own pointers to add.

Getting enough sleep

First and foremost, all the children go to sleep on time. And so do I! A well-rested family is the key to a successful morning. If I or one of the kids don't get enough sleep, everyone can feel it in the morning. We also straighten up the bedrooms at night. A neat room makes it easier and quicker for the kids to manage in the morning.

Waking up earlier

I set my alarm to wake me up fifteen minutes before everyone else has to wake up. Even if I'm tired, I push myself to get out of bed, and as soon as I start moving around, the tired feeling starts to disappear. Those fifteen minutes are precious. I get dressed, put myself together, *daven* the morning *berachos,* have a quick cup of coffee and then start breakfast. When the children wake up and see Mommy dressed and a nice breakfast prepared, they feel that everything is under control. I noticed that if I stay in my robe, there's a lazy feel to the morning and everything goes slower.

Varied breakfasts

Every morning I serve something different. I choose from a large variety for breakfast — eggs, muffins, hot cereal, bananas and sour cream, or, if I have more time, pancakes or French toast. If I'm running late, I serve cold cereal or crackers with a spread. The children are only allowed to sit down to breakfast when they're fully dressed with their hair brushed and shoes on. This works as a great incentive for them to get ready quickly.

Chani: That's pretty impressive, Sarah. I'm feeling like you belong in the *Balabusta* Hall of Fame! I, on the other hand, am a night owl, and it's hard for me to manage in the morning. My husband is the morning person in the family, so he's the one who sends everyone off to playgroup and school.

I prepare in advance so that things will run smoothly in the morning. My best trick is that I dress the younger kids in clean clothes the night before, so that my husband doesn't have to dress them! Aside from an unplanned accident in the middle of the night, this works very well for us. I also line up all the shoes by the front door the night before. *Dressing kids the night before*

My kids feel too rushed to sit down for breakfast, so I leave a box of whole wheat crackers on the kitchen table and they each grab a few as they leave the house. *Crackers for breakfast*

I keep my little girls' hair really short with bangs. It's not that I like the look so much, but it's worth saving my husband the time figuring out how to do their hair. *Short hair*

Dena: Doesn't it bother you when you wake up and see the aftermath of the morning?

Chani: Not really. By doing the mornings in this way, I am agreeing to let go. I can't expect my husband to do everything as I would do it. This is what works for me. I'm so grateful for his help that I don't let the little differences get to me. *Lower standards*

Dena: Tova, you must have some morning tricks! You're always so insightful when it comes to dealing with children.

Tova: Some of my children wake up super early. At one point, I tried everything I could think of to extend my night's sleep — I forced them out of my room and I tried all kinds of threats. Of course, none of that worked. The *Deal with reality* kids would wake up the rest of the household and everyone would start off the day in a bad mood. After many unsuccessful mornings, I finally learned my lesson and now I just get up with the early risers. I accept that my day has really begun with sunrise. Now that I have accepted it, it's easier to deal with. I started saving dishes to wash and laundry to fold for those early morning hours. I try to make time during the week to take naps to catch up on my sleep, because I don't usually manage to go to bed early.

Start the day positive

I've learned that the attitude and mood that the children get from me in the morning can make or break their entire day. I try to look away when they do something I don't approve of. If a child takes an unhealthy snack for breakfast, I make believe I didn't see. I don't want to send them off on their long day with a bad feeling of Mommy's disapproval. I'd rather prepare a better breakfast the next day.

Be solution-oriented

I do my best to teach my children how to deal with the morning pressure. Instead of allowing the hysterics to escalate over a lost shoe or an imminent bus, we work it through step-by-step to come up with a quick alternate solution.

Chessed by example

A lot of subliminal messages on doing *chessed* can be given over in the morning. I help them look for the missing notebook instead of lecturing them on being more organized. I'll fill up water bottles and prepare snacks for kids who are rushing, even though they're perfectly capable of doing it for themselves.

Discuss issues later

Lots of issues arise in the morning: children fighting, itchy tights, a bad hair day… I usually discuss these issues at a calmer point during the day. I'm a better listener and they are less hysterical when there is no pressure. We've come up with countless solutions together and avoided many problems in this way. I discovered that microfiber tights or a bit of hair gel can get the kids out fifteen minutes earlier and much happier. We have also worked out many sibling rivalry issues that take place in the morning by setting rules in advance. One of our important rules is, "No standing on anyone else's bed to reach your shelf." We now keep a step stool in the room to make it easier to keep this rule. There's no showering in the morning after a certain time, because it holds up the bathroom.

Dena: What an idea — setting rules in advance! At times I can feel my blood pressure rising as a child starts a meltdown in the morning and is about to miss his ride.

Tova: Dena, that happens to me, too! When it does, I mentally walk myself through the stages of the upcoming scenario. "So what is the absolute worst?" I ask myself. "So he'll miss his ride and I'll have to take him. I'll be a few minutes late for my doctor's appointment, but the doctor often runs late anyway. Maybe I can send him in a cab. I can really do that extra errand tomorrow. It's not worth exploding at him over something like this; he's also having a hard morning..." Talking it through in my head helps me calm down and enables me to help my child with what he needs.

Walk yourself through the scene

But thanks to everyone's suggestions, it sounds like I would have less to deal with in the morning if I set myself up better the night before. Maybe all these morning issues will become a thing of the past for our family, or at least, something that comes up infrequently. Ladies, when are we going to discuss evening routines?

Chapter 2

Evening Routines

Chani's Evening Fun Time

Chani: My evening routine with the little ones is an area that I'm confident in. My older children have busier schedules, and I'm unclear myself on how much leeway they should have. But I have the younger half of my family's evening down to a science.

Early baths   I often bathe my children before supper. The little ones need an activity anyway and they enjoy playing with our various bath toys. Two children together in bathing suits shortens the time and doubles the fun. Adding a little bubble bath to the water makes for a real treat! I find that giving baths early magically transforms the kids' moods from the action of the day to the tranquility of the evening. Once the children are sweet-smelling, relaxed and ready for bed, they feel that any remaining time they're awake is a bonus, and they make sure to stay well-behaved. *Baruch Hashem* they can't tell time! In the summer I bathe the children every day, since most of their activities are outside. In the winter, when they usually play indoors, then bathing every other day is sufficient.

Kid-oriented dinner   Right after baths, I serve dinner. I try very hard to sit with them so that they stay at the table and focus on eating their food. Sometimes, I may try to accomplish something in the kitchen, but I never leave. I learned from experience that leaving the kitchen during dinner only leads to disaster.

My goal at dinner is solely to ensure that my children eat, so I'm sometimes lenient in *how* I let them do so. These next ideas are unconventional and probably not worth bragging about, but some nights they're lifesavers, so I'll share them.

If I'm serving something for dinner that my children normally like to eat, but are fussing about that night, I will allow them to change locations and eat in a normally unacceptable place, such as in the hallway, on the stairs, under the stairs, or on the porch. For unwanted leftovers, I make a big plate of food for "myself" and I "allow" everyone to take turns eating off of Mommy's plate with their own forks. This turns undesired leftovers into the most popular food in the house!

Immediately following dinner, I lure them into their bedrooms by allowing them to eat their favorite fruit during our bedtime story. The fringe benefit is that no one can complain that they're still hungry before bed. Then we brush teeth and come back for bedtime songs and *Shema*. We all enjoy singing my personal composition thanking Hashem for our day and our family members. Truth be told, I put the little ones to sleep too early, before they're really tired, but I need my day with them to end, so that I have time and energy to give to the older half of my family. I leave the light on so that they can look at books in bed until they drop off to sleep. It can take over an hour.

Bedtime story and songs

Sarah: My kids would hop out of bed every two minutes if they aren't tired. Don't your kids come out and play when you're not looking?

Chani: Somehow, they know not to come out and play, but I do have a bit of trouble figuring out how many times to allow them to come out for a drink and the bathroom. Sometimes they "need" to come out of bed to get something and run right back in. I don't have any consistent rule and it gets me into trouble. Unfortunately, it usually depends on my mood and how cute they're acting!

Sarah's Rules and Consistency

Sarah: Here's where we differ. My two keys to a successful evening are enforcing rules and consistency.

Early dinner for younger kids

I feed the younger children early, around 5:00 P.M. That's when they're hungry and I prefer that they eat a meal rather than snack until dinner. In order to keep the atmosphere calm and the children seated at the table, I'll read them a short story, or, if I'm up to it, I'll play word games with them, like "I Spy," "What Rhymes With?" or "Twenty Questions."

In the meantime, my older children are doing their own thing — studying, spending time with friends, reading, etc. They're too busy to cut their afternoon short, and I don't mind if they grab a snack before eating a full meal. By the time they're ready for dinner, I'm finished putting the little ones to sleep.

Later dinner for older kids

The older kids eat dinner with me and my husband around 7:00. Serving dinner in shifts means more elbow space between children at the table, which of course cuts down on fighting. There is also less of a mess and I can focus on each child to make sure that they're eating. Once in a while, if my husband comes home early, we'll try to have a big family dinner, but it's not usually realistic because of everyone's schedules. Instead, we all look forward to Shabbos meals for family time.

Bath time is not play time

In my house, bath time for the little ones is very focused. Lots of playing in the bath usually means a pool on the floor, which is not for me. I also haven't found a successful way to store bath toys. They get moldy quickly and they're in the way, so I got rid of all of them. After baths, we brush teeth, cut nails (and check hair, if necessary) before we leave the bathroom. I also give fewer baths in the winter than in the summer.

After their baths, they are supposed to go straight to their beds and wait for their special time with me. I have the same routine with each of them separately, and they've grown to love it. We talk a little, I ask them about the best and worst parts of their day, and give them a relaxing rubdown on their backs. Their favorite part is when I "read their eyes." "Reading eyes" is my way of tapping into their hearts and planting goals in their *neshamos*. I'll say things like, "It says in your eyes that you enjoy doing *chessed* and that you are very *tzanuah*," or, "It says in your eyes that you tried very hard to share with your sister today," or, "It says in your eyes that you feel bad for kicking your brother." They often nod in agreement and are impressed with my correct assessment. Then we ask Hashem together to protect us and help us to be *tzaddikim* or *tzidkaniyos*. They get drinks and say *Shema*. They feel relaxed and satisfied and usually fall asleep quickly.

Private bedtime routine

When I'm finished with the younger children, I take a few minutes to refresh myself. This way, I feel put together when my husband comes home, and I'm ready for Round Two of dinner.

Transition to Round Two

Chani: I thought that I was just slow. It sounds like your evening routine takes hours, too!

Sarah: It definitely does. To manage dinnertime and bedtime correctly, giving everyone proper attention, usually takes me over four hours! I do have small pockets of time in between, so I use those to straighten up a little. Part of a successful evening routine is acknowledging that it actually takes that long!

Chani: I feel better. So how do you run the evening with your preteens?

Bonding with older children

Sarah: Dinner with the older children is actually relaxing most of the time. We eat together and hear about everyone's day. After dinner, everyone has an assigned job to do — clear the table, wash the dishes, sweep, wipe down the chairs, or clean up the toys. While the children take turns showering, I sit on the couch with one child at a time, and bond with him in some way. I find that during the day we are just too busy to connect, or the kids are too wound up from something that happened in school. But in the evening, when the children aren't running anywhere or doing anything special, they are usually very talkative, and I really try to take advantage of this unique opportunity. Even if I myself am cranky after a long, hard day, I try to connect with each child "on his terms" — in the way that he enjoys. For example, one child likes to read me stories while another likes to play games. I have a talented pianist who likes to perform for me before she goes to sleep. Another loves learning new things so we read a children's encyclopedia together. My husband puts the boys to sleep. He can bond with them in a way that I can't. He roughs around with them, tossing them in the air, tickling and wrestling with them. This doesn't seem to me to be such an appropriate way to put children to sleep, but I have been outvoted by all the boys, so I just look the other way.

Bedtime structure for older children

I'm sure some will disagree with my approach to bedtime for older kids, but I feel that structure is very important for them, too. They have two times that they are responsible for: prep time and bedtime. Prep time is when they are supposed to get into pajamas, brush their teeth and set up their books, clothes and other items for the next day. Any forgotten homework, test signing and whatnot has to get done during this time. Each child chooses, together with me, how many minutes before his actual bedtime he needs for his prep. Some children need fifteen minutes and some slower ones might need up to forty. We also decide on a bedtime together, based on how much sleep they need to wake up on time and according to their age. I try not to make their bedtime too early, because then it's too hard for them to fall asleep. They pretty much fall asleep as soon as they hit the pillow.

There are no consequences for missing prep time, but, if they go to bed more than ten minutes late, they have to go to sleep earlier the next night. I'm pretty consistent with my evening routine and its rules, so my children usually follow through.

Tova's Laid-back Routine

Tova: Your picture perfect evenings seem too good to be true! My family could never stick to such a rigid schedule. There is always something coming up that sets off my evening — a big test or paper that takes extra time, a bar mitzvah, an important phone call or a child with an urgent issue to discuss. My evening routine starts with dinner and finishes around 11:00 P.M., with a lot of action in between.

Dinner is served whenever it's ready for whoever is ready to eat. I aim to have it prepared by 6:00 P.M., but I'm not always consistent. I feed all the younger children and whichever older children are home and hungry. I always

Eating dinner together

make sure to sit and eat with them. A hungry mother doesn't give such positive vibes at bedtime. When the children see me enjoying my dinner they are more inclined to eat nicely.

Complimenting and sharing

When I can, I use the opportunity to have the children practice good *middos* by asking each child to give individual compliments to everyone at the table. I feel so proud when I hear them mimic compliments that I've given them in the past. Sometimes, I'll share an interesting experience or a special *siyata diShmaya* that I merited that day. They enjoy when I make the effort to share my day with them.

Keeping dinner available

The food stays on the stove for the rest of the family. If the older children missed the family dinner, they can eat whenever they are ready as long as they serve and clean up after themselves. I'd like to be there to serve every child, but on a practical level, it just doesn't work. My husband's schedule is also unpredictable. He often has to stay out late or has a *simchah* to attend. I want him to feel welcome whenever he arrives, even if I am in the middle of something. I set a nice setting for my husband at the table with an appetizing food arrangement on his plate, complete with a pretty napkin and microwave dish cover. I'm ready to greet him whenever he shows up.

My children don't like bathing, so I limit baths to three times a week. That's the minimum.

Biological bedtime

After dinner time and bath time, we start bedtime. None of the children have a time written in stone. I start the bedtime routine with the youngest, and keep going until I'm done! Somehow, it works out that each night they go to sleep around the same time. After they reach *bar/ bas mitzvah* age, I don't tell them when to go to sleep, since they find it insulting. I discuss with them proper sleeping habits and how much sleep I think they need. They choose their bedtimes according to what their bodies require. Those discussions seem to have paid off; recently my older daughter surprised me by choosing a bedtime earlier than the child under her, since she has to wake up earlier to travel to school.

Sarah: An older child going to sleep earlier than a younger one — that would be a public embarrassment in my house.

Tova: It works in our home because it makes sense to the kids. They also want to function in the morning.

Chani: My kids would totally abuse such a privilege.

Tova: If I see that they are abusing it, we discuss what's not working and why it's not working. I point out how their crankiness, intolerance and inability to study are due to lack of sleep. They usually tighten up their schedule on their own when I make them aware of the problem. They appreciate the respect and space I give them and they want to keep it that way.

In the evenings, I don't try to get the house cleared out and quiet in order to have my own time. I actually do quite the opposite: I make myself available between 7:00–11:00 P.M. for all my children. I don't have anything else I plan to accomplish during those hours, and I try hard not to go out too often in the evening. The evening is my time to get in touch with my family's lives in a way that works for them. If I miss bonding with a child one night, for whatever reason, that's okay because I'm on top of the situation. I'll make sure that they get ample time the next night. The times I do have to go out, I get *nachas* hearing

Nights are for the family

how some of the kids filled my role, inquiring about each other's day and giving their siblings warm feelings at bedtime.

Dena's Pointers

Dena's no-phone zone

Dena: Your homes sound so serene. My house must have gotten all the extra doses of *kvetchy*, misbehaving, overtired children to balance out the neighborhood!

No one here seems to need any advice on bedtime. I'll just mention a few points that haven't been brought up yet. First of all, I disconnect the phones for a few hours in the evening. I'm surprised no one has mentioned this basic deterrent to a successful evening.

Staggering dinner time

In my family, each child takes only five to ten minutes to eat, so I stagger dinner time and call them into the kitchen one at a time. There is no fighting at all and I can deal with each child's food fussiness according to my own criteria. This is especially helpful with leftovers. For example, all the children love matzah balls but will eat soup without it. I have only one child that insists on matzah balls, so I reserve that for him without the others noticing. One child will finish up the *cholent* if there are no better options. It's sneaky, but mothers are entitled! Hopefully no one tells on me.

Anticipating bedtime issues

Before they get into bed, I try to anticipate every conceivable excuse my children will use to come out of their bedrooms. Every child has his own *shtick*, and I try to address them all, from kissing the *mezuzos* three times to checking under the bed for snakes before we say *Shema*. Even if it means sitting with them in their rooms until they fall asleep, it's worth the extra time, since this insures that the evening runs smoothly. I make up stories, sing songs and often fall asleep with them. They are usually pretty tired and fall asleep relatively quickly.

I walk my husband to night *seder* when I can. The time spent together outside the home is so important and refreshing. And it's more private than trying to talk at home.

Time with your spouse

My last tip is a "must-do" for every mother after birth. I hire a teenager to be a mother's helper for two hours every evening. She holds the baby, puts the other children in pajamas, and is basically my extra pair of hands for the evening. I keep her on until my baby's moods and schedule becomes more reliable. This really makes this particularly challenging time a lot more manageable.

New baby

I so enjoy that moment, after checking in all the bedrooms, when I see that everyone is sleeping soundly in their beds. The night is still young, and I have a lot to do before morning!

Quiet time at night

Chapter 3

Preparing for the
Yamim Nora'im

Realistic Self-Improvement Tips

Dena: Rosh Hashanah is in just a few weeks! I'm so busy at work and with getting my kids organized for the new school year that I just can't schedule in the time to focus on the upcoming *Yamim Tovim*. When I do find a free moment, all I want to do is just cook and stock the freezer. I wish I could find the time to sit and concentrate on preparing for Rosh Hashanah in *ruchnius*.

Learning practical halachah sefarim

Back in seminary, I used to love reading *machshavah* and *mussar sefarim*. It was so inspiring, and I miss it. Nowadays, when I do make time for enhancing my *ruchnius*, I'll sooner pick up a *hilchos Shabbos* book or go through the latest English explanation of the *Shemoneh Esrei*. I don't have the time to wait for inspiration — I need to brush up on *halachos*, so that I'm sure I'm keeping the *mitzvos* properly.

Tova (sighing):   Yeah, I know what you mean — exactly! During Elul, I really try to listen to Torah *shiurim* when I have a lot of dishes to wash or a large load of laundry to fold. It's a great way for me to get a shot of inspiration from the best lecturers without sacrificing my housework responsibilities. I don't do it often, though, because it slows me down a bit. I'd be happy to lend you some really great CDs that you can listen to while you're driving to work.

Dena: Thanks, Tova. During the month of Elul, I always have this unsettled feeling in my heart that I'm missing a special opportunity to work on myself.

Tova: I can relate! I'm also so busy with so many different things, especially since it's the beginning of the school year. Between getting all the school supplies and books ready, shopping for school and Yom Tov clothing, setting up appointments, cooking for Yom Tov, adjusting to everyone's new schedules and needs for the year... And that's besides the regular laundry and meal routines! Then we have two birthdays in Elul... Between it all, I don't have a minute to think. Wouldn't it be convenient for Rosh Hashanah to come at some point during the winter after all the kids already adjusted to their new teachers and everyone is basically running on auto-pilot? Then I could sit down with a *Mesillas Yesharim*!

I don't believe that Hashem expects me to drop my responsibilities, and learn *mussar* and say *Tehillim* half the day in preparation for Rosh Hashanah. But I did come up with something really manageable to make my Elul more meaningful. It has really worked for me.

Every Elul, I pick two small things to work on — one *bein adam l'chaveiro* and one *bein adam laMakom*. I pick something very small and very doable. This year my *bein adam l'chaveiro* is to make sure to give my kids detailed compliments about something nice that they did that day. My *bein adam laMakom* is to be more careful that my skirt shouldn't ride up when I step in and out of the car.

Choosing two small things

Dena: That's it?! That's your preparation for Rosh Hashanah?

Tova: Yes! I don't have the time to be so spiritual and lofty, and even if I would make the time, I don't always have the head for it. By picking something very important, yet small, it's easy for me to work on it for the whole month of Elul. Since I'm consistent, by the time Rosh Hashanah comes, I'm not embarrassed to stand before Hashem on *Yom Ha-din*.

Dena: Wow! That actually is pretty lofty, but it's also very doable. Do you have any other suggestions of small areas to work on that are just as easy?

Tova: One year, my *bein adam l'chaveiro* was not to get annoyed when someone cut me in line at the store. Another year, it was to have my husband's dinner hot and on the table as soon as he walked in the door. One time, I tried to learn two *halachos* of *shemiras ha-loshon* every day. Another time it was to ask a certain needy neighbor of mine if she needed me to pick up anything for her at the store.

For *bein adam laMakom* — I'm always trying to sneak in a good time to learn a *halachah* a day. I'm always surprised to find out how many *halachos* I don't keep perfectly or never even knew. I've tried learning one every day at breakfast, at dinner with my kids or every time I sit down to nurse the baby. Keeping the *sefer* next to the rocking chair helps. One year, I took on a *kabbalah* to stand still while saying *Asher Yatzar*. I've taken on different *hiddurim* in *hilchos* Shabbos. It's not hard to find something small to improve on that fits into my day.

Dena: These sound like great ideas, but the truth is *kabbalos* never really worked for me; I don't really know why. I feel bad about it, too.

Making proper kabbalos

Sarah: Don't be so hard on yourself, Dena. It may be that you're just picking something impractical for your lifestyle or schedule. I'll tell you the formula I've learned about taking on *kabbalos* that works for me.

1. I pick something that is absolutely doable and then do half of that.
2. I always write down the *kabbalah* in a notebook to make it more real.
3. I set a time to review it on a regular basis, like on *motza'ei* Shabbos or every Rosh Chodesh.

Dena: What kind of things do you do?

Sarah: Small! Very small! Having *kavanah* in the first *berachah* of *bentching* only when I eat bagels. Not raising my voice with my kids just on Sunday mornings. Adding one more part of *Pesukei D'Zimra* to my *Shacharis* once a week. The idea is to pick something small enough that it won't be hard to keep up. I master it completely and then it's mine! I feel I'm doing something to further my *ruchnius* and it keeps me going. I do this just for Elul and if I see it was successful, I try to keep it up the entire year.

Chani: I have a different approach completely. During Elul, I try to work on my mindset and focus on proper *hashkafos ha-chaim*. I don't like picking specific things to work on. I get too caught up in my checklist, and if I fall short, my sense of self-worth goes down the drain.

Working on your mindset

Sarah: What do you mean?

Chani: During Elul, I work on focusing on my awareness of the fact that Hashem loves me. Even if I yelled at my kids and even if I *davened* without thinking, Hashem sees all my efforts and my spiritual desires all of the time. He cares about me and wants me to succeed. Focusing on these ideas helps me grow closer to Him. It helps me deal with the challenges that come up during the day instead of complaining about them. Hashem arranged my day's events so that I can grow from them. These ideas help me live with Hashem, make *berachos* with more *kavanah*, do more *chessed* and appreciate the good in my life.

Tova: You never take on specific *kabbalos*?

Chani: Here and there I do. But mostly, the changes in my *avodas Hashem* come as a result of strengthening positive *hashkafos* in the house. This Elul, at suppertime, I'm asking each of my kids to write down something good that happened to them or a special *siyata diShmaya* of that day in their own memo pad. On Shabbos, we all read our memo pads at the table. We do things like that to build the feeling of living with Hashem.

Cheshbon ha-nefesh

I also got into the habit of making an unofficial *cheshbon ha-nefesh* at night as I am going to sleep. I think about the different areas that I know I need to work on and make a mental note if I have advanced in any area. I don't like writing things down. I try to focus on a positive self-image. I compliment myself a lot. Writing things down eventually ends up as a negative experience for me.

Reconnecting with mentors

Another important and meaningful thing I do in Elul is strengthen my relationships with some of my mentors. A call to the *Rebbetzin* or a past teacher to wish her a good year is not only appreciated by them, but great for me. I get in a question or two, and try to drink in the proper *hashkafos* and attitudes from their answers. I find that when I associate with the right people, the proper *middos* and values become part of my life through osmosis.

Sarah: You know, it never occurred to me to strengthen myself and my home in that way. Calling my old mentors would do wonders for me. I'm so glad we spoke about this.

Technical Tips for Cooking

Dena: You all seem to be so solid in your *ruchnius! B'ezras Hashem* by me. I can help you in the technical aspects of preparing for Yom Tov. I am super organized in my cooking at this time of the year. Some years there are just so many days of eating! Two to three days of Yom Tov with Shabbos in between, the *seudas mafsekes*, meals to break the fast, *erev* Yom Tov food... It doesn't stop! I couldn't possibly cook that much at one time even under the best of circumstances.

The way I manage will probably sound a bit extreme to you all, but it's the only way I can successfully satisfy everyone's diets, taste buds, and my own need to be creative in the kitchen.

I have three stages of cooking before Yom Tov. The first one is in the summer during my vacation.

Three stages of pre-Yom Tov cooking

Chani: The summer! You cook for Rosh Hashanah in August?

Dena: What can I do? That's when I have the time. Remember, I'm a working mother. I use this time to make time-consuming dishes that I feel are essential to our Yom Tov meals. I have a huge deep-freezer and I organize everything individually by the shelf. I keep a list on the door of what's in there. In August, I make babkas, soufflés, stuffed cabbage, round challahs, prepare frozen cookie dough, and a few more complicated side dishes.

Stage two is after the kids are back in school, before the pressure at work starts. I set aside two to three afternoons or evenings as official cooking days. I make all of my family's standard favorites. One day I make cakes: mandelbrodt, apple cakes, chocolate cakes and cookies. On another day I prepare meats: meatballs, chickens, roasts, chicken soup and matzah balls. I also make some potato kugels just for *erev* Yom Tov. At this stage, I take a good look at my work schedule and compare it to the Yom Tov calendar to figure out which days will be the hardest to prepare for, and then I cook for those days too.

Chani: So you finished cooking for Sukkos already?

Dena: Partially. I can't afford to do one Yom Tov at a time. This is stage three: About a week before Rosh Hashanah, I make a master three-week menu which includes Rosh Hashanah, Yom Kippur, Sukkos, *chol ha-moed, erev* Yom Tov and all the meals in between. I include all the foods that are already in the freezer. I decide what to serve when and I see what's missing from the menu. This is when I take a few minutes to go through some recipe books in order to incorporate a new interesting dish or salad into our Yom Tov meal. I have the time to juice up the menu because all of my basics are already done. In order to save time when I'm ready to prepare these new recipes, I write the title of the recipe book and the page number I need on my calendar.

Scheduling the last week   After I write out this three-week menu, I make a complete shopping list and cooking plan, according to my work schedule. I make a schedule so that I can fit in everything that still needs to get done — cooking the few dishes that can't be frozen, making the salads and taking care of odds and ends. Of course, there's also all the regular laundry and household chores.

Chani: It sounds like you found a way to reduce a lot of the last-minute pressure for yourself.

Dena: Preparing for Yom Tov in this way allows me to provide for all my family's needs, still go to work and also enjoy Yom Tov myself. By the way, this method is also helpful for holidays like Purim, a one-day holiday packed with so many details. I always pick a few aspects of the

Purim preparations and take care of them way in advance. Costumes are an easy one to do early. *Mishlo'ach manos* can be done pretty early, too. I save my lists from year to year so that I know exactly which supplies and food I have to buy.

Tova: Wow, Dena. You are an *aishes chayil*! I don't think I could do what you do, but I could probably implement your ideas on a smaller scale. I'm thinking that when I cook for a regular Shabbos in the summer, I can double some recipes. It would be great to fill up the freezer and take some pressure off the *erev* Yom Tov cooking marathon. That bit of extra effort in the summer really would help a lot.

I have a tip for the extra, unplanned-for Yom Tov meals, like *chol ha-moed* Sukkos suppers. On *chol ha-moed* morning, I put up some sort of chicken and potatoes dish in the crock pot. When we come back from our all-day activities, the food is hot and ready to be served. What a treat!

Using a crock pot

Helpful Ideas for the Days of Rosh Hashanah and Yom Kippur

Dena: How about some ideas for the days of Rosh Hashanah and Yom Kippur themselves? It's important for me to have a somewhat spiritual day and get a little more than my usual *davening* in. I've tried giving the younger kids a new toy to keep them busy, but their playing usually doesn't last more than a half hour, an hour tops. Between the obligation to hear *shofar*, having to fast, and all the *davening*, I find these days very hard to manage with the little kids. Anyone have any good tips for me?

Davening early

Tova: My husband *davens* at the *vasikin minyan* on the Yamim Nora'im, which begins before sunrise. By the time he gets home, I can still catch a lot of *Musaf* and *shofar* blowing in *shul*. On Yom Kippur, this schedule is particularly good because when he comes home after *Musaf*, it's still early in the day. This way, I can usually get to lie down for a few hours until he goes back for *Minchah* in the regular *minyan*.

Some years, instead of my husband going to *shul* before sunrise, I wake up for *vasikin*. Either I go to *shul* or just *daven* at home before the kids wake up. Of course, I *daven* for *siyata diShmaya* to be able to *daven* without interruptions. To *daven* so early in the morning, the very first moments of the new year — there is no *davening* experience more special than that! When I do this, I don't even feel the need to go to *shul* to experience Rosh Hashanah.

Feeding the kids early

On Rosh Hashanah, I make sure to feed my kids lunch before *shul* is over. They can't wait that long! As for Yom Kippur, I make sure to have the foods that my kids like available. I set it up so that it's easy for them to serve themselves. I leave the hot plate on so they have warm food, and I leave all the plastic ware on the table for them. If I'm up to it, I help serve them. I also buy a lot of yogurt and string cheese, and I make sure to have homemade healthy muffins available. When their hunger is satisfied, they're more relaxed and better behaved.

Toy exchange

Chani: This is what I do to keep the kids busy on the Yamim Nora'im: On *erev* Rosh Hashanah and again *erev* Yom Kippur, I do a major toy and book exchange with a good friend or relative. I borrow five to ten toys that my kids don't have and a ton of books. I hide them all until the moment before I plan to *daven*. Then I pull out two toys and a few books, present it to them and start *davening* immediately. I figure that I have at least twenty minutes, hopefully more. One year, the kids played for an entire hour! All through the day, any time I need to *daven* or when the children get antsy that Abba is still not home from *shul*, I keep pulling out new toys and books. I do have to be careful and watch that they do not ruin anything, but it's worth the effort.

Of course, there's always the traditional *pekalach* that never fail to do their magic. When I don't have interesting toys handy, I give my kids larger than normal size *pekalach* before I am about to *daven*. I explain to them that this is a special treat for them to eat, as long as they behave while Mommy is *davening*.

Snack bags

For the most part, on Rosh Hashanah and Yom Kippur, I try to just work on my *middos* while watching the children. My job is not to be in *shul* all day, but to take care of my kids. My older girls help me as much as they can, but they also want to *daven* in *shul*, and they're also fasting. I find that Yom Kippur is a good time to start giving some younger children the opportunity to be a little bit more helpful. They are not fasting and they understand the urgency of the help on Yom Kippur.

Having younger children help

Sarah: I usually take turns with a neighbor for Rosh Hashanah *davening*. She watches my kids and I go to *Shacharis* and then I watch her kids and she goes to *Musaf*. The next day we do the same, but in reverse order.

Taking turns with a neighbor

The times I'm home by myself with my kids, I try to take care of every imaginable problem that can come up before I start *davening*. I supply them with toys — on separate sides of the room! — provide snacks and drinks,

Anticipating problems beforehand

and make sure they've gone to the bathroom. Then I start *davening* and hope for the best! I'll never forget: One time after I did this, my three-year old had an accident on the floor while I was *davening Neilah. Neilah!* What could I do? I left my *Shemoneh Esrei* and took care of my son and the mess. This is my *avodah* of the day. Let me be *mekabel* it *b'simchah*, accept it happily. Isn't that the best thing that I could offer Hashem on such a holy day?

Chapter 4

Maintaining Daily Ruchnius

> *Note:* There are various opinions concerning women's obligation to *daven*. Please ask your own Rav before relying on the suggestions below.

Finding Time to Daven and Having Kavanah

Finding the time

Tova: Over the years, I got stuck in a bad habit where I just couldn't find the time to *daven*. It was so easy to rationalize and say, "I'm a busy Mommy! Aren't mothers of little children exempt?" And it was really true — I simply didn't have a quiet moment to *daven*. "I should be sleeping after being up all night with the baby! I need to put my messy house back together. I have to cook, do laundry, make important phone calls that can't be put off. Who could *daven* anyway with a curious toddler and a baby crawling around the house? Hashem understands!" There was always something pressing for me to do. I would say *birchos ha-shachar* and go about my day. This went on for a long time; I convinced myself that I couldn't find even twenty minutes in my morning to *daven* an acceptable *Shacharis*.

Dena: I can totally relate! But Tova, you're so into your *davening* now. What changed?

Tova: I reached a stage where I was so overwhelmed with all the children's needs, my needs and the chores building up everywhere. I was unhappy with a lot of things in my life, and I didn't even know how to begin to climb out of the stress that was building inside of me.

Understanding the importance

Around that time, I happened to go to a *shiur* about the importance of *tefillah*. The *Rav* completely changed my attitude towards *davening*. He made an important point that really hit me hard. I'll say it over in the way that I internalized it: "I feel I don't have time to *daven* because I'm so busy doing such important things. But that's exactly why I can't afford not to *daven*. Hashem is the *Kol Yachol*—He can do anything! He is the Master of all that happens in this world—including everything I need to get done today, big or small, my success as a wife, a mother, everyone's health, our *parnasah*, getting the laundry done and toilet training my two-year old! All this can only happen successfully if Hashem wills it. If I make the time to ask for help, I will have more time, and the details of my day will work out. I'll have more *siyata diShmaya* and more successes."

I realized that I had to make *tefillah* so important to me that I couldn't feel it was optional, and make time for it just like I'm always able to make time for other things that I feel are important.

Dena: So what did you do?

Tova: I slowly worked *davening* back into my busy mornings. I gave myself pep talks to stop what I was doing and pick up my *siddur*. "Only Hashem can make my day run smoothly," I would tell myself. "Maybe the baby can eat a snack in the high chair while I give it a try." I put *tefillah* at the top of my priority list, even on days that I thought it was impossible to find the time. *Making the time*

I am now very careful not to make phone calls or start any significant activity of my morning before I *daven*. If I'm nursing or expecting, I say *berachos* and eat first to give me the strength before I start. *Davening before anything else*

To get myself going, I try to envision myself *davening* back when I was single and had all the time in the world. I really grew in my connection to Hashem then, and made *Connecting to positive experiences* a solid *kinyan* in *davening*, so I try to recapture that feeling now that I need some extra inspiration.

Seeing results   I notice that the days that I manage to *daven Shacharis* go much smoother and I accomplish more. This motivates me to continue. I am now at the point, *baruch Hashem,* that if I don't *daven,* I feel the lack in my relationship with Hashem and see the lack of success in my day.

Connecting through the text   **Sarah:** I have a different problem. Being very structured and organized, I can almost always make the time to *daven.* My problem is connecting to Hashem through the words of *Pesukei D'zimrah* and *Shemoneh Esrei.* It comes much more naturally to me to connect to Hashem through my own personal *tefillos* all day long. That's where I feel the main part of my relationship lies — asking for my needs. "Hashem, please let the baby fall asleep so that I can get some work done! Hashem, please let my daughter sit still for the dentist! Hashem, please help me make the right decision for this child." I'm happy with my relationship with Hashem throughout the day, but it bothers me very much that I don't achieve the same closeness through the *Shemoneh Esrei.* I'm always trying to think of different ways to work on it.

Tova: What have you done?

Making davening a priority   **Sarah:** I've committed myself to making *tefillah* a priority in my day. I do something similar to what you do. I *daven* first thing in the morning, after the kids leave. I try my hardest to resist throwing in a load of laundry or washing the breakfast dishes before I *daven.*

I also have special toys that I give the baby or other kids (if they're around) that they get to play with only when Mommy is *davening.* When I'm finished *davening,* I put the toys away so that they remain exciting for the next time.

If I'm running out early one morning to an appointment or to a *bris*, I try to figure out the night before when I'm going to *daven*. Either I'll wake up early or I'll make sure that there's a time slot designated for *davening* later in my morning. Otherwise, the day will just fill up with the usual stuff and I will have lost the opportunity to *daven* that morning. I try not to *daven* on a bus or in the car. It makes me feel as if I'm trying to squeeze Hashem into my day.

Planning davening time

Another thing I've tried is to take out a minute or two a day to learn a few *halachos* of *tefillah* or to read some inspiring words about *tefillah*. There are many books on the market that can be used, and I found the ones that work for me. Learning about *tefillah* on a regular basis, even for such a short amount of time, has definitely made a difference in my *kavanah*.

Learning about tefillah

I've made myself a comfortable set place to *daven*, a *makom kavuah*, in the living room, and sometimes I use my husband's *shtender*. Knowing that I am showing Hashem that *tefillah* is a priority for me gives me *chizuk* even if I'm not connecting, as I would like, through the words themselves.

A set place for davening

I always keep in mind a *mashal* from the Chofetz Chaim of a lady who was walking through the market and dropped an entire basket of apples. The apples were quickly rolling away out of reach. As fast as she could, she grabbed the ones she could still get to, and put them back in her basket. She lost most of them, but at least she had salvaged a few for her family to enjoy. When I catch myself not paying attention in the middle of *Pesukei D'zimrah* or

Grabbing what you can

Shemoneh Esrei, I try to grab as much *kavanah* as I can at that moment, focusing on the sentence that I'm up to, and "put it back in my basket." I don't give up.

Reviewing the translation

Dena: Wow, you all have some great ideas for working on *tefillah*! Here's my idea, tried and tested: When I *daven*, I try to focus on the literal meaning of the words. The words in the *tefillos* are very powerful. I'm able to tap into them if I make the effort to read them and understand them, instead of just reciting them.

Sometimes, I see that I am repeatedly getting stuck in a certain section of the *davening*. When that happens, I try to take the time to pick up a *sefer* and read a *peirush* on that section. This helps me intellectually, and it stimulates more *kavanah*. I am grateful that I feel motivated to do this.

Sarah: I like that idea. I review the *halachos*, but never tried reviewing explanations. If you have a favorite *peirush*, I'd love to borrow it or get myself a copy.

Birchos ha-shachar out loud

Dena: The truth is — I'm a big talker! I don't usually have the time in the morning to properly dedicate to *Shacharis* the way I described. I do try to wake up extra early, but often my kids wake up when they hear me, and then I'm not able to *daven*. But I do always make sure to *daven birchos ha-shachar* at home before I leave. I want my children to see that *davening* is important to me, and I enjoy when they answer Amen to my *berachos*.

Davening Minchah

Since I don't always have a proper *Shacharis*, I am very careful to remember to *daven Minchah*. As soon as that quiet lull in the afternoon rolls around, I don't start folding laundry — I *daven Minchah*!

Chani: What "quiet lull" in the afternoon? I haven't noticed any of those lately! I don't have any great advice about finding time to *daven*, but this is what I do to help with *kavanah*: I discovered that focusing on my problems when I was *davening* was not productive. When I would start giving Hashem my laundry list of all the areas that need His help, my problems would overtake my thoughts and distract me from *davening* properly.

Focusing on appreciation

So, instead, before I start *davening*, I try to focus on the things that I'm grateful for. All the good things in my life that Hashem has granted me — like, my wonderful family, our good health, my home, good relationships that I have, food on the table, and successes I've experienced. Once in a while, I even make a list to pull out during *Modim*. When my daughter had an eye issue, I added to the list, "Thank you Hashem for letting my eyes work without any problems." When my son split his head open, I wrote, "Thank you Hashem that this doesn't happen more often!" I've even thanked Hashem for creating vitamins, and other things in my life that I could easily take for granted.

Of course, when I feel I am in need of His help in a particular area, I do have it in mind when I *daven*. I keep a list of my requests and every few months make note of how many of my needs have been addressed! This gives me *chizuk* and fills me with *hakaras ha-tov* which, of course, enhances my ability to *daven* with more *kavanah*.

Dena: How much time do you give yourself to *daven*?

Chani: It's hard to say. It really depends on ... well... everything! On Rosh Chodesh, I make sure to have a nice long *davening*. This way, I know that at least once a month,

Special Rosh Chodesh davening

I invest a significant amount of time and energy into my *davening*. I try not to schedule any appointments on those mornings. I really connect to the *pesukim* in *Hallel* and I sing most of it out loud.

Tova: Your ideas are very inspiring, Chani! Everyone here seems to be saying that treating *davening* with importance on a regular basis is the best way for a busy mother to get her daily dose of *ruchnius*. I'd like to move on to the rest of the day. I believe that we have opportunities to connect to Hashem all day. I prefer not to just leave Hashem in the *siddur*. Does anyone have any other ways of connecting themselves and their families to Hashem throughout the day?

Being a Source of Ruchnius for Your Family

Starting and ending your day

Sarah: I picture my day as a sandwich. The "bottom bread" is my morning — starting my day on the right foot by waking up on time, washing *negel vasser* next to my bed, getting dressed quickly and *davening berachos* right away. The "top bread" is my evening — learning my *shemiras ha-lashon halachah*, saying *keriyas Shema* and going to sleep on time. Keeping this proper structure uplifts the whole "filling" of my day, whatever it may be. Starting and ending my day correctly keeps me focused on the right *hashkafos* during the day.

Tova: You still keep up with learning *shemiras ha-lashon*?! How do you do it?

Shemiras ha-lashon

Sarah: Various organizations have come up with so many innovative ideas for reviewing *hilchos shemiras ha-lashon*.

Every year I pick a different one to keep me and the family interested. I have a calendar with a different *halachah* and illustration for every week hanging over the kitchen table. We discuss the week's *halachah* every so often. There are also *shemiras ha-lashon* index cards. One year I put them in a *bentcher* holder and hung them on the wall. Every day we pulled out another one to learn. This year, I joined a program that gives tests on the *halachos* twice a month. I learn a little at night before I go to bed. Opportunities to be careful in *shemiras ha-lashon* come up all day long. Raising my family's awareness of the *halachos* has been a fabulous way to build the level of *ruchnius* in my home.

I also try to instill *ruchnius* by making parties for my kids — Shabbos parties, Rosh Chodesh parties, *berachos* parties, etc. I find that creating a fun event is a great way to instill positive *ruchnius* experiences into the home.

Mitzvah parties

Every once in a while, my husband and I open a *sefer* together. It's a nice springboard to discuss *hashkafah* and strengthen our values and goals together.

Learning with your spouse

I'd love to hear what the rest of you have to say.

Dena: I pick one *sefer* a year on the *parashah* or another topic that interests me and learn it thoroughly.

Choosing one sefer

Sarah: When on earth do you find the time?

Dena: I don't know — here and there. It really does take a whole year to finish one *sefer* properly.

I also make sure to give some change to *tzedakah* every day. I always keep in mind what the Rambam says: It's not how much money you give that's important, but how many times you do the action that makes an impression on the *neshamah*. This small mitzvah that I do every day makes me feel much more connected.

Giving tzedakah

Saying Tehillim

Saying *Tehillim* keeps me feeling connected to Hashem. I keep a pocket *Tehillim* with me, and I use it whenever I'm stuck waiting somewhere or on extended hold on the telephone.

I try to share all these little things that I do with my children, to let them know that there are always opportunities to do *mitzvos*, even when we're busy.

Sharing stories with kids

Chani: I also feel it's important to share with my children. I do this by telling or reading them stories. Often I'll tell them personal stories — how I saw *siyata diShmaya* in my day, or about a struggle that I had in my *middos* and how I tried to overcome it. I find that stories are a good way to subliminally give over the attitudes and aspirations that I would like to instill in them.

Appreciating nature

I'll tell you something that's personal if you promise not to make fun. I have plants and flowers all over my house; I admire a flower's beauty and a plant's awesome symmetry. When I look at a stunning flower I think, "Hashem created this beautiful flower for no other reason than to bring beauty and happiness into my life." I watch the flowers bud, blossom, grow, die and then bud again, and this heightens my awareness of the wonders of life and the beauty of creation. Being surrounded by them infuses me with this message every day of the week.

Tova: You know I never thought about plants in that way. I never even bought any real plants for the house because who has time to tend to plants when you're tending to children?!

Elevating household duties

To keep me feeling spiritual throughout the day, I try to make a conscious effort to elevate all my household duties, for example, by thinking, "This clothing that

I'm washing is worn by the precious *neshamos* that You gave me to care for," and, "Let the food that I'm preparing be nourishing and satisfying to my family and give them strength to go about their day." When I prepare for Shabbos, I often think of how women are compared to the *Kohanim* in the Beis HaMikdash. The *Kohanim* did very tedious work — *shechting* animals, preparing *korbanos*, baking bread, and yet there is nothing more spiritual than the work that they did! I try to feel the same way about my own Beis HaMikdash.

Maybe with all these ideas for infusing my home with *ruchnius*, the floor of *my* Beis HaMikdash will also miraculously absorb all the dirt and spills of the day's work without a washing!

Winter —
Kislev, Teves, Shevat

Chapter 5

Shabbos

Preparing for Shabbos Efficiently

Relieving erev Shabbos pressure

Sarah: The responsibilities of a large family are *bli ayin ha-ra* too many to make all of our Shabbos preparations on Friday. I invested a lot of time brainstorming on how to relieve some Shabbos pressure by doing things earlier.

The following description is how I would ideally like to prepare for Shabbos. Without a thought-out plan, I go into Shabbos very stressed and unsettled. I try very hard to achieve the perfect *erev* Shabbos scenario, but I must admit that I don't always get to every detail of my system. My plan of action consists of four points.

1. Freezing in advance

A deep freezer is a must by me. I couldn't run my home without it. I make all my chickens at once, every two months or so, I place a big order and have all my sauces, spices, tins, and freezer space ready. If the chickens are frozen, I defrost them all and clean them (hopefully with the help of a family member). I then season all the chickens at the same time, a few of each kind, bake them and freeze them in separate tins, so I can pull each tin out when I need it and heat it up easily.

When I buy fresh chickens, I spice them immediately, and then put them in the freezer. I can then defrost and bake them fresh on Friday. I separate all the necks and wings and make huge pots of soup, which I also freeze with matzah balls. I sometimes freeze the fresh chicken parts in small packages for soups to be made at a later date.

Many other Shabbos food can be frozen as well. I bake challah once every 3 weeks, and *kishke* once every two months. Whenever I can find some extra time any day of the week or month, I cook and freeze, so that when

Shabbos approaches, much of the food is already made.

Apple, carrot, zucchini and noodle kugels, cookies and cakes all freeze beautifully. I even freeze potato kugel, and reheat it straight from the freezer, open, in a very hot oven. I always try to make a few kugels and cakes at the same time, while all the ingredients are already out and handy. It saves me future time and energy.

If I don't have time to bake that extra cake, I'll double the dry ingredients only, put the extra mixture in a plastic bag, and store it in the fridge. This way, I've got my own "ready cake mix" — I only have to add eggs and oil and I have a cake. This is especially useful for those last-minute *shalom zachor* cakes!

I wrap all my food very well, either with strong plastic wrap, good plastic bags, sealed containers, or with generous aluminum foil. Everything comes out delicious! We call it "fresh frozen" in our house.

Many of my friends claim that they can't imagine a Shabbos without "fresh food, straight out of the oven." I feel that it's not worth the inevitable stress. There are so many other important details that go into making a successful Shabbos that I prefer not having to worry about last-minute food preparation.

Whatever is left to cook or prepare for Shabbos, I do on Thursday. I even peel potatoes for the *cholent*, and let them sit in a pot of water in the fridge, until I prepare the *cholent* fresh on Friday. Sometimes I even prepare the rice with spices, oil, mushrooms and water on Thursday, to be cooked fresh on Friday. *2. Cooking on Thursday*

Cooking on Thursday means preparing a menu in advance and shopping for all the ingredients early in the week. The big advantage of doing this is that when I cook

I don't waste precious time searching for ingredients. I rotate the same basic recipes that my family enjoys from week to week, so it's really not difficult to decide what to make.

To keep my kitchen constantly functional, I clean up as I prepare each dish, washing dishes and pots, and putting ingredients away. The clean countertop helps me feel calm and prepared.

I enlist the help of some of the children to clean up toys, books and general clutter on Thursday night, so that all the cleaning is not left for Friday.

Friday is for last-minute cooking preparations that could not be done before — like preparing fresh salads, washing the kitchen floor, straightening up, bathing all the children and resting before Shabbos.

3. Calm Fridays I try to maintain a calm environment when my children come home from school on Friday. It is certainly counterproductive to be greeted by a frazzled mother who has no time for them. I make sure to greet them properly, *shmooze* with them about their day, look over their schoolwork, and hang up their pictures. This sets the tone for a calm and relaxed *erev* Shabbos.

We have a pretty set schedule for Friday afternoons. After we eat lunch, the younger children shower and take naps or read in bed. The older girls prepare salads or read books and the boys ride their bicycles. When all the children know what is expected of them, there is greater potential for the day to run smoothly.

The most important thing that I provide for my children on *erev* Shabbos is food! I prepare filling and healthy foods — cut up vegetables, potato kugel, meatballs or chicken and whole wheat cookies for a snack. My children get very cranky when they are not fed adequately and the negative atmosphere this creates can spoil the aura of Shabbos, even before it starts.

I'm conscientious about taking care of myself during the *erev* Shabbos preparations. I enjoy speed walking for the exercise and fresh air. A forty minute walk with a friend on Thursday nights and sometimes on Friday, is a great outlet for my excess tension, and gives me the fresh air and exercise I need. Also, eating healthy, full meals both on Thursday and Friday is really important. When that doesn't happen, I treat myself to a special snack that I enjoy; a huge cinnamon Danish usually does the trick! Lastly, I try to get in a nap on Friday.

4. Something for myself

I almost always manage to do at least two out of these three things before Shabbos arrives. Not only is doing this beneficial for me, but my whole family benefits from having a happy and energetic mother on Shabbos.

Of course, the most important ingredient in a successful Shabbos is to *daven* for it. I include a special heartfelt *tefillah* that my Shabbos preparations should go smoothly and that my *middos* should stay intact. I always notice the difference when I *daven* for *siyata diShmaya*.

Chani: That sounds like a great four-step plan, but I personally don't think that I can keep up with all of its details. Having a freezer stocked with food is one of my dreams. Maybe I'll try it some day. Here are a few tips that have been helpful for me when preparing for Shabbos:

Setting the table Thursday night

I set my table for Shabbos on Thursday night. This accomplishment keeps me feeling on top of things even though nothing else is ready. When I'm running late on Friday, I look at the beautifully set table and feel calm.

Baking and menu shortcuts

When I'm baking, I save time by not washing out the mixing bowl and mixer between batters. More or less, the same ingredients are going right back into the bowl, so why bother?

I have a four-week Shabbos menu plan in my computer. I print out a menu Thursday night and zip over to the store to buy the ingredients. This way, I don't have to waste my time thinking, and I can get straight to cooking on Friday.

Shabbos fresh from the oven

Tova: I like having all our food fresh on Shabbos, so I plan the end of my week in a way that gives me time to cook on Friday. It adds a special flavor to our Shabbos table. To accomplish this, here's what I do:

I place a vegetable order on Wednesday. I do everything else on Thursday: bathe the children, go shopping, clean the house and take a nice long nap.

My time on Friday is planned wisely. I keep a running list of what I want to get done and by what time it should be accomplished. I start my cooking marathon, crossing things off my list as I finish them.

To keep my children occupied while I'm cooking, I often have a special activity or art project planned for them. The older children either help me with the cooking or with the little ones.

I enjoy having my children see the effort that I put into the Shabbos *seudah*. I like to believe that it instills a love of Shabbos in them.

At some point, when the activity has lost its excitement, I announce — often in desperation! — that it's rest hour. As Shabbos draws near, everyone has to rest, read books or play quietly in their rooms so that I can finish up the last-minute details.

I am constantly giving myself pep talks on Friday to stay calm with the children. I don't think it's really possible to have a completely calm *erev* Shabbos with such a large family and so many things to do. As long as my *middos* stay intact and I light candles on time, I consider it a successful *erev* Shabbos.

Dena: Here's what I do to put together a nice Shabbos despite my busy schedule.

Shopping by phone

First of all, I don't go to the supermarket. I order all my groceries via fax or email and have them delivered to my door.

I am also a big freezer person. I couldn't survive without it. During my summer and winter vacations, I stock the freezer with basics that my family likes, such as kugels, cakes, meatballs and *kishke*. Since the basics are taken care of, I have time every week to add special touches to the Shabbos meals.

Of course, there's still plenty left to do besides the basics. So on Thursday nights — and I know this doesn't work for most people — I stay up until 3:00 A.M. cooking for Shabbos. By the time I go to sleep, I'm finished with practically everything. I like cooking when the house is quiet, and when I have a lot of time on my hands. Since I don't work on Fridays, I catch up on sleep in the morning.

Staying up late Thursday nights

I try to prioritize which foods I'm preparing and which I'm buying. I make the chickens myself because it's a lot more expensive to buy ready-made chickens. I enjoy taking the time to make challah myself and getting the mitzvah of *hafrashas challah*, so I make that a priority. On the other hand, I buy pre-cut salads and if I'm running low on frozen kugels, then I'll buy that, too.

Prepared foods and other shortcuts

My greatest discovery has been the "cooking bag." I always use one in the crock pot and in Pyrex dishes. They can be transferred easily from the oven to the freezer to the hot plate, they save space in the freezer, and best of all, using them saves on cleanup time.

My *erev* Shabbos meal is my family's favorite: frozen pizza with a side of popcorn. It's just so easy and convenient — everybody likes it!

Bringing in Shabbos on time

Here's the tip I'm most proud to offer: *bentch licht* twenty minutes earlier than calendar time. When I manage to do this — and I do! — I greet Shabbos like a *mensch*, welcoming Her in properly. And if I don't manage, I still have the extra twenty minutes leeway to finish up, and I'm still able to light candles on time.

Shabbos Table Tips

Treats, toys and parashah desserts

Tova: The goal of our Shabbos *seudah* is to make it as sweet as honey. Ironically, the more I lower my expectations, the more successful our *seudah* is. Here are some things we do to encourage a warm and happy Shabbos *seudah*: Children who sing the loudest and nicest get treats. Younger children get special Shabbos *seudah* toys after they eat; this helps them stay in the vicinity of the table.

I often make desserts connected to the *parashah*, like a cake in the shape of Noach's *teivah* or red jello for *makas dam*. Or I'll make a picture in the cream on the cupcakes — a ladder for Yaakov Avinu's dream or pictures of *keilim* from the Mishkan.

Coping with rowdiness

I leave the "flow" of the meal to my husband. He picks up on the needs of the moment and chooses to speak, sing, or talk, depending on everyone's moods. At some point in the meal, the kids get a little too rowdy. Instead of scolding them or sending them away from the table, I myself leave the table and relax in my room for a few minutes. I started doing this when I noticed that no one else minded their behavior except for me!

On *erev* Shabbos, I make sure the kids eat a healthy meal so that I don't have to pressure them at the *seudah* to eat their chicken. I don't focus on manners or nutrition at the Shabbos table. This may sound too carefree, but I don't want my Shabbos meals to resemble the meals of the rest of the week.

Keeping a pleasant atmosphere

At the end of the Shabbos meal, I announce everyone's achievements in *middos* and *ma'asim tovim* that I kept track of all week, but didn't necessarily mention. We all congratulate each other's successes; this makes for a wonderful family bonding experience.

Sarah: Our Shabbos *seudah* runs pretty differently than yours. I devised a terrific seating chart for the Shabbos table, carefully separating siblings who tend to fight with one another. Every meal we rotate clockwise, so that every child gets to sit next to either Mommy or Abba at some point during Shabbos.

Seating charts and meal breaks

We have specific time slots designated for *divrei torah* and *zemiros*, and we've allotted recesses in between for children to play. The children know that their free time will come soon so they have more patience when they're at the table. Some kids can't sit still no matter what, so I use play seatbelts to remind them what I expect.

I guess my family is used to more rules, so this system really works for us.

Parashah competition

We also have a wonderful Torah Bee for the entire family with questions on the *parashah*. My husband asks questions on all age levels and we use an open Chumash to answer. This keeps everyone interested in staying at the table.

Simple and kid-friendly

Chani: I'm happy to report that keeping my kids at the Shabbos table is not such an issue for us. First of all, I only make foods the children eat and enjoy — nothing too fancy. The kids don't eat fish, so I don't make it. Our standard favorite menu is: plain roast chicken, rice, roasted potatoes, Israeli salad, and blondies for dessert.

I also keep lots of interesting spices on the Shabbos table. This is an easy thing I do to make the Shabbos table different. This way, the kids can spice up the food the way they enjoy it, with no effort on my part.

My husband chooses a nice story from one of the children's books series and reads it at the table. We ask one or two questions from everyone's *parashah* sheet. We don't burden the rest of the family by reading through the entire page they get from school.

Keeping the meal short

Dena: I like the sound of your relaxed meal, Chani. What we do in order to keep the meal pleasant is to keep it moving quickly, so there's no time for fights! *Kiddush, Ha-motzi,* food, *zemiros,* Tatty's *divrei Torah,* dessert and *bentching.* When we have guests, we add to this routine a bit.

The children tell us their *divrei Torah* privately at some point over Shabbos and not at the Shabbos *seudah.* Their siblings are really not interested in listening to anyone's *derashos.*

We leave *shmoozing* and story telling to the afternoon. My husband and I take turns getting in our Shabbos naps, and that's usually when my husband tells his famous stories. His stories are a big hit with them — the younger children enjoy his theatrics, while the older ones try to discover the *mitzvos* or lessons that can be learned from the story. And I enjoy my much-needed rest!

Shabbos Guests

Dena: *Hachnasas orchim*, having guests, is a priority for us. I put a lot of thought and effort into figuring out how to have Shabbos guests fit into my own busy schedule and that of my family. My basic approach is to do something extra for my guests to make them feel comfortable and special, but not to disrupt my own routine and lifestyle. *Fitting it in*

I prepare the guest room as early on in the week as possible. It's always an added pressure that looms large, so I make sure to get it done early. We purchased extra comfortable mattresses for our guest room, so after I've made the beds, I feel like I'm well on my way in honoring our guests.

Preparing some food for my guests to eat on *erev* Shabbos is part of my Friday routine. Guests usually arrive hungry and whatever I prepare gets eaten! If I don't have time to make a kugel, I put frozen knishes or bourekas in the oven; they go over almost as well. *Making guests feel at home*

I have no expectations of my guests to help. If they offer and I feel their offers are sincere, I do give them a job to make them feel at home.

Our meal is a balancing act between maintaining happy children and entertaining guests. I make sure that even when we have guests, the menu consists mostly of kid-friendly foods: chicken cutlets (*schnitzel*), rice, *cholent* *Including the kids* and chicken soup. Then, I add an interesting dish or salad per meal that I think my guests will enjoy. My kids won't touch it, but it's fine since they're still getting their favorite dishes.

We want our children to enjoy the mitzvah of *hachnasas orchim* and not feel left out, so we've patented our own method to accomplish this. After the appetizer, we have all the guests and family members introduce themselves, say where they're from and describe the highlight of their week. We find this method to be a comfortable way for everyone to meet each other and a creative way to keep both children and guests involved in the same conversation. After the kids go to sleep, we sit with our guests and focus just on them.

Making it work

Chani:　We don't have company too often, but when I was growing up, my parents had company all the time. My mother is able to have guests often without turning the mitzvah into a burden, because she keeps everything very simple.

She serves the exact same menu every week. This routine has enabled her to make Shabbos so smoothly that she could prepare it in her sleep.

My father often barbeques the chicken on the grill outside and my mother makes a gefilte fish roll, rice, potatoes, string beans, *cholent* and an easy salad. Sometimes, she makes a potato kugel and in the winter an easy vegetable soup. That's enough food for the whole Shabbos.

If the guests ask what they can bring, she always asks for dessert. The guests feel good that they are contributing, and she's able to cross it off her list. My mother even has her guests set the Shabbos table. This makes them feel useful and good about coming. Of course, it's also helpful to my mother.

She always keeps pareve ice cream in the freezer and a supply of chocolate syrup, just in case dessert doesn't show up.

When my husband and I do have guests, I make it easier by using nice paper plates instead of real dishes. I often let them set the table. I find that this easy but important task helps the guests feel more comfortable in my home. Using paper goods makes the cleanup a lot more manageable.

Using disposables

During the meal, my husband is in charge of entertaining the guests while I make sure to tend to the children. This division of jobs allows everyone's needs to be taken care of properly so that the meal runs smoothly.

Splitting responsibilities

Sarah: We also don't have guests very often. We find Shabbos to be a special time to focus on the children. Having guests changes that dynamic for us.

Buying the extras

When we do have guests, I keep to my regular menu and I buy some extras — interesting spicy salads, kugel, deli and a cake. I'll also defrost an already-prepared chicken and add more potatoes to the *cholent*. Buying the extras allows me to enjoy having guests without the burden of all the time-consuming preparations.

Tova: My husband is a real people person and he loves having guests. I enjoy the occasional adult interaction also, but it's hard to really tap in to that when the kids need so much attention. So we compromise and have guests about half the time. I've learned that guests don't need fancy foods or table settings in order to enjoy themselves. They enjoy the warmth of our Shabbos table, the friendliness

Keeping priorities straight

of the kids, and the Shabbos flavor in the food. All this I have plenty of! So I don't need to do much extra in terms of preparation. There is extra cleanup of course, but that's not a big price to pay for the many benefits of having Shabbos guests.

Shabbos Checklist

It's a good idea to check this list twice on Friday — once in the morning and again closer to Shabbos.

- ☑ Challah
- ☑ Grape juice/wine
- ☑ Appetizer
- ☑ Main
- ☑ Side dishes
- ☑ Salads
- ☑ *Cholent*
- ☑ Dessert
- ☑ Shalosh Seudos
- ☑ *Erev* Shabbos foods
- ☑ Nosh
- ☑ Soup Nuts
- ☑ Tea essence
- ☑ Hot water urn
- ☑ Open packages and bottles
- ☑ Defrost food from freezer
- ☑ Rip toilet paper
- ☑ Rip paper towels
- ☑ Rip tin foil
- ☑ Open diapers
- ☑ Put away *muktzeh* toys
- ☑ Heaters/fans
- ☑ Check for clean Shabbos clothes/socks/tights
- ☑ Iron shirts
- ☑ Check that *eruv* is up
- ☑ Separate yogurts (if applicable)/open cans
- ☑ Make sure that light in fridge is off
- ☑ Set Shabbos clocks, alarm systems
- ☑ Hot plate/*blech*
- ☑ Heat liquid foods

Chapter 6
Menu Planning

Making Planning Painless

Dena: I have to share with you a tough time I went through, and how I worked my way through it. As a working woman, I really don't have so many hours of my day to devote to cooking and housework. On the other hand, I enjoy preparing healthy and delicious meals. I see it as a way that I can shower my family with love.

As my family grew and my hours at work became more demanding, I began to feel a knot tightening in my stomach every afternoon as mealtime approached. "Supper, again? Didn't we just eat last night?" I would quickly think of something wholesome to prepare only to find that I was missing some key ingredients. The kids would start getting antsy from hunger and I would find myself reaching for a bag of noodles again, or making a side dish of hard-boiled eggs to accompany a package of frozen veggie burgers. That may pass as a meal once or even twice a week, but I went a little overboard. This went on for quite a while. I finally took hold of the reins and decided to plan out my meals and shopping schedule ahead of time, taking the many factors of my life into consideration. It took some time, but I succeeded in making meal planning painless, practical and enjoyable.

Sarah: Please share your ideas with us; I'm always looking for new ideas, especially in this area of never ending meal preparation!

Planning a weekly menu

Dena: I'll tell you what I try to do. On *motza'ei* Shabbos, I sit down and plan out my menu for the entire week. Each week has its own special time considerations, depending on my work schedule, doctor appointments, and other irregularities in my week. I plan easier meals for the days I come home late, or have a project to work on at home.

I take into consideration the family members who don't like to wash for bread twice a day, and only serve bread one meal each day. I also try not to repeat recipes twice in one week, in order to keep the menu inviting and interesting. As far as the nutritional aspect, I make sure to keep our yellow cheese intake down to twice a week, fried food down to a minimum, and processed meat (like hot dogs and salami) down to once a month.

For dinner, I basically mix and match five types of proteins and five types of carbohydrates.

It has taken me time getting used to the European/Israeli meal schedule. Since the kids come home from school early, I find that I need lots of extra menu ideas for lunches. In order to keep things interesting, but not too complicated, I keep to the same basic menu with slight variations every week.

Lunch: Variation of same basic menu

For example:

Sunday lunch is pancakes, but every week I make a different kind — whole wheat, fruit or cheese.

Monday lunch is tuna fish — tuna melts, sandwiches with lettuce and tomato, tuna casserole or croquettes.

Tuesday lunch is pasta — ziti, lasagna or spaghetti.

Wednesday, I serve cheese sandwiches — cheese with mayonnaise, mustard and baco-bits are a big hit in my family. I also make pizza on Wednesday.

Thursday is egg day — scrambled, sunny side up or omelets.

Friday lunch, we eat up all the leftovers!

I usually cut up sticks of cucumbers, carrots and wedges of tomatoes to ensure that everyone also gets plenty of vegetables. Knowing which category of food I'm serving for lunch every day has removed so much tension from menu planning, yet also leaves me room for some spontaneity.

Mixing and matching **Sarah:** That's a great lunch plan, but my main issue is dinner. What are the five types of proteins and starches that you mentioned, Dena?

Dena: I choose from chicken, ground turkey or meat, chicken cutlets or shwarma, fish, or cheese. I mix and match these with five different carbohydrates — potatoes, rice, pasta, quinoa, and bulgur for a variation. I often use potatoes twice a week and skip one of the more unusual grains. For pasta, I vary between orzo, couscous and others.

Combination dishes that save time   Another trick I picked up along the way is that I try to combine at least two food groups[1] into one dish. My beef-a-roni recipe is my favorite because it combines three — grain, meat and vegetables. I find that preparing salads are very time consuming. So instead, I make sure to get vegetables into the main dish, like spinach lasagna, meatballs and cabbage or vegetable pizza. When this doesn't work out, I'll prepare a salad. During the day, my kids snack on fruit.

Keeping it simple **Chani:** Sounds delicious. I'm coming over to your house to eat! In our house I keep meals very simple. My kids have a few basic dinners that they like and I make them all the time. I serve Shabbos leftovers on Monday instead of Sunday to give them a "day of rest." I cut up a simple salad

---

1. The five food groups are: Grains, Fruits and Vegetables, Dairy, Meat and Protein, Fats and Oils.

and I'm finished. Lunch everyday is either noodles, eggs or some sort of sandwich on whole wheat bread. I have the same basic shopping list every week, because nothing by me usually changes. My best tip for an easy and nutritious meal is a filling soup.

Dena: Doesn't it take a lot of time to cut and peel all those vegetables?

Chani: No, not at all. I came up with a real time saver. Don't laugh — I scrub all the vegetables really well and just throw them into the pot uncut. Even if I'll be pureeing the soup, I'll leave the peels on. But I can only do this if I remember to start the soup early on in the day, because the vegetables need more time to cook. When I serve it, I use the ladle to cut off chunks of vegetables for each bowl of soup. I serve it with yummy whole wheat rolls or fresh bread. Because I make the same things all the time, I usually don't have trouble preparing meals. I guess it gets a bit boring, but at least there's good food to eat!

Your menu sounds so delicious and interesting, Dena, but too detailed and complicated for me to handle.

Dena: It's really not difficult at all. Having planned out a menu in advance, I save so much time, energy and stress over what I'm going to serve for my next meal. I keep a very well-stocked pantry. I do a huge shopping once a month, filling up on all my standard ingredients in addition to my meat products. After making my weekly menu on *motza'ei* Shabbos, I then write my shopping list for all the fruits, vegetables, eggs and milk products that I need for the upcoming week. By being so organized, I'm usually never without an ingredient that I need, and my stomach doesn't go into knots before every meal.

Major monthly shopping

Sarah: Wow! Sounds too good to be true. When do you find the time to cook such wholesome meals?

Finding time **Dena:** If I know I have a long day at work, I'll try to prepare a little the night before, or even quickly in the morning before I leave. I'll mix the tuna, spice the chopped meat, mix the pancake batter, or peel the potatoes. Those few steps done ahead of time make things go much more smoothly later in the day when I'm under pressure with hungry children all around me. Sometimes my husband comes home for his lunch break, and either he or the babysitter makes lunch with my pre-prepared ingredients, and my instructions.

I make dinner in the late afternoon with the kids at my side. I've learned to be pretty quick in the kitchen. Nothing I make takes more than twenty minutes of actual busy time. Even if the kids are unhappy or fighting, I just putter around the kitchen until I'm done. Timewise, it helps a lot that I don't have to think about what to make.

Finicky Children

Overstocked pantry **Tova:** I have a different approach than both Chani and Dena. I think it has helped me deal with the very common issue of finicky eaters. I don't have an official weekly menu. I work off a subconscious one in the back of my head. I enjoy cooking very much. I have about fifty different spices in my spice cabinet and I am always experimenting with new tastes and recipes. Since I never know what I'll be making for the next meal, I try to keep an overstocked pantry so that I won't get stuck without the ingredients I need.

Sarah: Fifty different spices! I didn't even know there

were so many! We're a salt and pepper family. I splurge with garlic and paprika sometimes. Your kids try new foods on a regular basis?

Tova: I'll tell you my approach. First of all, I've elimi- *Something for* nated foods that all family members don't like, like fish *everyone* and green leafy vegetables. Second, whatever I'm making, I make sure that there is something for everyone. If I know a particular child dislikes chopped meat and I'm making meatballs, I make sure that there is a side dish that they do enjoy. Most of the children eat most of what I prepare, most of the time.

I never banish a dish from my menu completely, be- *Keeping* cause I never know when the kids will eat it again. You *a variety* never know with children! One night they'll love a new *available* recipe that I tried, so naturally I'll be quick to make that dish again. Of course, the next time, the same child won't touch that very same dinner and he'll announce his opin- ion loud enough to discourage the rest of the children! I find that as they grow, their taste buds are constantly changing. My three-year-old used to hate chicken, but ever since she turned four it's been her favorite food. Her body must know that she needs it.

The key is to offer a variety of tastes from the time *Training their* they are very young — as soon as they start to eat table *palates* food. This trains their palates to remain open to variety. I enjoy flipping through cookbooks, and I try one or two new recipes every week. Since I do this often, eventually everyone tries something new.

Another trick I find very useful is to serve the food *It's all in the* in an attractive manner. Sometimes, I'll change the look *presentation* of the table with a different fold of the napkin. Other

times, I'll make a face out of vegetables on top of a casserole or put a pretty radish flower on top of a spread or
salad. These little touches take no time at all and will often make the difference in the number of tasters I have.
My younger children appreciate the nice presentation of
food, as well as the attractive table settings, as much as
the adults do.

Not getting
offended   Finally, I don't get hung up on the kids not liking what
I made. I'm perfectly comfortable with giving a child a
bowl of healthy cereal, crackers with a spread or a sandwich as a substitute every once in a while. I try hard not
to be confrontational with them, but I do plan my menu
to make sure that this doesn't happen more than once or
twice a week for each child.

Lately, I've been much more health conscious and I
have been trying to come up with new recipes that include
healthier grains. Unfortunately, I think I've started too
late, since my children have been protesting more than
usual. Any good ideas?

Including Healthy Foods in Your Meals

Chani: I may cook simple, but I definitely try to cook
healthy. I'll share with you some practical tips I've come
up with.

Whole wheat
breads   Whole wheat pita goes over better in my house than
whole wheat bread. I make pita pizza on whole wheat, as
well as falafel with salad or spicy whole wheat zaatar-
spiced triangles. They also enjoy fresh whole wheat rolls,
French toast and cinnamon toast. There are so many different kinds of whole wheat breads to choose from besides

the standard loaf. No one by me will eat a plain whole wheat sandwich.

I mix whole wheat noodles with the plain white noodles, covered with a thick pasta sauce and cheese so that the whole wheat noodles are not so noticeable. I do have one child that goes fishing just for the white noodles, but the rest seem fine with it. I started off with a low ratio of whole wheat to white noodles and I gradually increased it to fifty percent without the kids complaining. I also use whole wheat couscous and orzo, which the children really enjoy.

Whole wheat noodles

I hide whole wheat flour in a lot of foods. I only use a hundred percent whole wheat flour in my chocolate cakes and cookies. The kids have no idea because the brown color of the whole wheat flour is masked by the chocolate. There are two tricks to successful whole wheat baking. You have to add an eighth to a quarter more liquid per cup of flour and it cannot be overbaked at all. I tried different recipes and different types of whole wheat flour until I came up with ones that worked for me. There are many kinds of whole wheat flour on the market. Many people I know like the seventy percent whole wheat mixed with thirty percent white, that's ground extra fine for a less dense result, but I usually just buy the regular whole wheat flour and mix it myself with white flour. It is much more economical.

Whole wheat flour

There are many whole grain cereals and crackers out there that are delicious. These are a great way to incorporate healthier grains into the family diet. I do make sure to choose crackers low in saturated fat. My kids take these as snacks to school. Oatmeal is also a child-friendly grain that is extremely healthy. It works well in cookies, as a soup thickener or can be especially enjoyed as hot cereal.

Other grains

I use wheat germ to decorate many baked goods and challah, and I add it to yogurt and sandwich spreads. The kids think it looks pretty. Unfortunately, my kids don't like bulgur or quinoa, which are extremely healthy, but I continue to try different recipes for these.

Sarah: My kids just can't be fooled! I don't know how you do it.

Setting a good example

Chani: I think the clincher is that I try to set a good example for them. I'm always eating my whole wheat bread and salads in front of them and I make sure it looks appetizing. I also discuss with them why eating healthy is so important. I teach them how sugar slows down your immune system and gives you false energy; how whole grain flour is more easily digested by the body and provides the body with many more nutrients than white flour. All these ideas have eventually seeped in over the years. Of course, I don't have these discussions as I am about to serve a meal — that approach would definitely backfire!

When we talk about food choices, I offer my kids options. I ask them which kinds of healthy foods they like the best and when they like eating them. We also talk about new foods and when they would be willing to try them.

Sarah: How do you get your kids to eat vegetables?

Fresh and cooked vegetables

Chani: I'm blessed that my kids all enjoy a fresh salad. Sometimes I'll hide some cooked vegetables in my pizza sauce — puréed carrots, sweet potato and zucchini are all disguised very well in the tomato paste. I'll often make a yummy dip and put it in individual *schnapps* cups next to each person's plate. The carrot sticks and pepper strips are eaten much faster that way. I also experiment with different salad dressings. One of my children started eating tomatoes and another one cabbage as a result of trying a new kind of dressing.

Tova: I've seen some interesting recipes in the book, *Deceptively Delicious*, by Jessica Seinfeld, on how to hide puréed vegetables in almost any food, such as, pancake batter, bread crumbs, chopped meat or mashed potatoes.

Sarah: You all have some great ideas. I hope my children will go for them.

Meal Planning in a Crisis

Sarah: When I spent time in the hospital with a family member, I just didn't have time to make meals. Take-out food was not an option on a daily basis, due to the expense. We ate a lot of processed frozen foods from the freezer, but that was also costly, besides not being very healthy. I only had one afternoon a week to get my act together. I hired an older girl to help me and we spent the afternoon making tons of my family's favorite meals — lasagna, pancakes, French toast, chicken with rice, meatballs and anything else that could be frozen. I made sure to have all the ingredients that I needed in advance. The babysitter defrosted one meal each day and my family ate the foods they liked and felt taken care of even though I wasn't physically there for them. We also got help from neighbors and family, but it was nice not to be solely dependent on them.

Hiring cooking help

Chani: I wonder if I could get through bed rest during my pregnancy like that. I could sit in a chair and direct someone around my kitchen once a week, in order to prepare for the entire week.

Sarah: I know someone who manages just like that on a regular basis. She has a very large family and wasn't managing to keep up with all the cooking and housework. Cleaning help was too expensive, so instead, she hired a teenager for relatively little money, to cook all the meals for the week in one afternoon. In that way, she freed up the rest of her week for all the other household chores. I thought it was such a brilliant way to save money and still get the necessary help to keep her home functioning.

Cooking extra for Shabbos

Tova: Last summer when we made a *simchah*, I was particularly busy for a few months and couldn't keep up with the cooking. I used to prepare a lot of extra food when I cooked for Shabbos. It was easy once I was already cooking to make enough food to last for the week. We ate "leftovers" all week long. I also changed the presentation so it didn't look like I was serving leftovers. I tried changing the name to "rightovers"!

Well-balanced meal

Chani: As long as all is well, I aim to feed my kids two well-balanced meals a day. Sometimes when things get difficult, like when I'm on bed rest, I just aim for a well-balanced day! They don't have to eat from all the food groups at every meal, do they? During a really trying month, I try to look at the larger picture and aim for a well-balanced week. If I overdid it on the pasta one day, I'll try to even it out with proteins and vegetables the next day. I do the best I can under the circumstances and *daven* that my children should grow up strong and healthy. As much as we teach our kids to eat healthy, health comes from Hashem, not spinach. Isn't that the bottom line?

Sandwich and Lunch Ideas

[Sandwiches]

- Pareve hot dogs sliced in circles + ketchup. Can be eaten at room temperature or prepared in a sandwich maker.
- Whole pareve hot dogs + roll. Can be eaten at room temperature or prepared in a sandwich maker.
- Sour cream, cream cheese or *gvinah levanah* (Israel) with any of the following: Dill, garlic powder, olives, fried onions, sliced tomato, jelly, cucumbers, green onion (scallions), olives in toaster oven.
- Yellow cheese + ketchup. Can be eaten at room temperature or prepared in a sandwich maker. (Optional: pizza spice/olives)
- Pita pizza. Can be prepared as a closed sandwich in a sandwich maker or open in the toaster oven.
- Yellow cheese with spices
- Yellow cheese with mayonnaise
- Grilled cheese. Prepare in the morning and wrap in aluminum foil)
- Tomato sauce and olives + bits of cheese
- *Chumus* plain, with spices, olives or with pickle packaged separately
- *Techinah*
- *Techinah* + honey
- Eggplant spread + chopped cucumbers
- Homemade cream cheese
- Butter and garlic powder toast. Can be made in a sandwich maker.

- Ketchup and salty cheese
- Triangle cheese spread over butter. Easier to spread on frozen bread.
- Cottage cheese and ketchup
- Cottage cheese + ketchup + pizza spice in sandwich grill. If kept in long enough, it will melt like yellow cheese.
- Cottage cheese plain
- Toast
- Almond butter
- Peanut butter and jelly
- Peanut butter and chocolate spread
- Mexican peanut butter (spicy—with hot pepper!)
- Peanut butter and sprinkles
- Tuna and pickles
- Butter + cut up vegetable of choice
- Omelet in a sandwich
- French toast
- Toast with butter + cinnamon and sugar (try with whole wheat)
- Zaatar toast (try with whole wheat)
- Veggie burger (pareve *schnitzel*) with ketchup. Whole or sliced in sandwich maker. You can make a few sandwiches with one sliced burger.
- Rice cakes with favorite spread or plain
- Carob spread
- *Challah* rolls with a piece of chocolate baked inside
- *Challah* rolls with a pareve hot dog inside

- Plain roll

- Mayonnaise + sliced hard boiled egg

- Whole wheat crackers + olive spread

- Whole wheat crackers + ketchup

- Sandwich alternative: Hot oatmeal in a bowl, wrapped in foil,

- Sandwich alternative: Cereal in a bag, milk in a thermos + plastic bowl and spoon

[Lunches]

- Spiced baked potato halves + cottage cheese+ sliced peppers (Dip halves in oil & spice mixture, bake face down on baking paper.)

- Baked potatoes with butter and/or slice of hard cheese to melt inside after baking + *leben*/yogurt + cut vegetables

- Vegetable sticks (cucumbers, pepper, carrots, tomatoes, other) + two different dips e.g. *chumus*, white cheese spread (*gvinah levanah*) or sour cream and onion soup mix + healthy crackers (every week a new kind)

- Oatmeal + fruit

- Carrot muffins + cottage cheese + sliced peppers

- Green apples + peanut butter + yogurt + crackers

- Brown rice with cinnamon and sugar + yogurt + fruit

- Homemade granola with milk

- Pita with falafel (frozen balls/fried from mix/fresh from store) + salad + French fries (frozen package) + *chumus* + *techinah*

- Homemade pizza on pita or with any dough
- Pita pizzas with personal toppings, such as, onions, peppers, corn, and olives (You can disguise cooked vegetables ground up in sauce.)
- Eggplant parmesan
- Lasagna
- Noodles with cottage cheese
- Noodles with white cheese sauce
- Mixed white and whole wheat noodles + tomato paste, pizza spice, a bit of yellow cheese, spoon of brown sugar, milk and a container of cottage cheese
- Orzo with onion soup mix sprinkled with cheese (Buy grated cheese and use very little; kids feel like they ate a yellow cheese meal.)
- Tuna noodle casserole
- Tuna melts (Tuna + bit of yellow cheese + sliced tomato, baked open in toaster oven.)
- Tuna sandwiches + salad + pickle
- Tuna-potato casserole
- Tuna loaf
- Tuna patties
- Scrambled eggs (omelets on bread/rice cakes) + *leben* + salad
- French toast (This is a great way to use whole wheat bread.)
- Egg pizza (Giant egg and cheese omelet with ketchup, cut in wedges.)

- Pancakes (whole wheat/cottage cheese/yogurt)

- *Matzah brei*

- Whole wheat cottage cheese cupcakes/muffins + apples

- Fresh whole wheat bread from bread machine with spreads and sliced vegetables (cream cheese, tuna, cottage cheese)

- Bagels + spreads + vegetables

- Leafy salad with feta cheese (salty) + zaatar toast

- Tomato soup and bread (brown rice in soup)

- Blintzes (Fry leaves, prepare different fillings for kids to add themselves — cottage cheese with sugar, mashed potatoes, or other.)

- Egg salad sandwiches

- Cereal and milk

- Veggie burger and bread/orzo

- Pareve hot dogs in roll or bread

- Fish burger + couscous

- Veggie burger + couscous

- Assorted french fries — potato, sweet potato, zucchini + tuna salad

- Sweetened large container of sour cream (cocoa and sugar) + fries and ketchup

- Dairy *lukshen* kugel

- Tuna noodle salad

Dinner Ideas

[Poultry]

- Chicken stir fry: Use leftover cut-up chicken, sautéed onions, mushroom, peppers, zucchini, soy sauce and spices, served over rice.
- Chicken breast with cauliflower and broccoli
- Drumsticks and rice: Spice and bake on 400° for an hour and a half until crunchy.
- Chicken cutlets: Fry or bake fifteen minutes on each side, serve with potatoes or rice.
- Chicken soup with vegetables, noodles and chicken in soup
- Roasted chicken with vegetables
- Grilled chicken breast + salad + Israeli couscous
- Sautéed chicken bites: Cut up cutlets, spice with paprika and granulated garlic, and fry in oil. Serve with Israeli couscous and salad or in pita.
- Chicken salad and bulgur
- Broiled chicken wings: Marinate in olive oil, red wine, lemon juice, garlic powder and paprika. Broil fifteen to twenty minutes on each side.
- Sesame chicken nuggets with a sweet sauce
- *Shwarma*: Turkey cubes with fried onions in a pita + french fries
- Orange chicken: Sauté cut up cutlets with vegetables in an orange juice sauce.
- Barbecue chicken

- Turkey wings or necks with lentils cooked with rice or potatoes

- Goulash: Cook potatoes, carrots, and turkey strips (*shwarma*) or cubed meat in one pot.

- Turkey stew with mushrooms and onions

[Ground Meat/Turkey]

- Meat Bake: Sauté meat and onions till brown. Add spices and egg. Pour over cooked rice or couscous and bake.

- Meatballs and spaghetti/mashed potatoes/rice

- Hamburgers with lettuce and tomato

- Meatloaf

- Spaghetti and meat sauce

- Sloppy Joes

- Shepherd's Pie

- Meatballs and cabbage

- Meat patties: Fry a lot of onions, and cook meat patties in the fried onions.

- Stuffed peppers (with meat and rice)

[Deli]

- Deli sandwiches with lettuce and tomato

- Omelet with sautéed deli pieces

- Lettuce salad with deli pieces

- Deli slices rolled around a pickle with crackers or rice cakes

[Fish]

- Fish sticks + mashed potatoes

- Salmon: To pan fry, use non-stick Pam (olive oil) and sear fish on high heat.

- Salmon in vegetable sauce

- Nile perch, tilapia, or other fish, prepared with mayonnaise, soy sauce, mushrooms, served with mashed potatoes

- Tuna baked potatoes: Scoop out inside of already baked potato, mix with tuna and mayo and salt. Refill and sprinkle with paprika. Re-bake fifteen minutes.

- Tuna Chow Mein over rice

- Tuna croquettes + soup

[Soups]

- Vegetable soup + bread/toast/healthy muffin

- Minestrone soup + bread/toast/healthy muffin

- Pea soup with or without meat/hotdogs + potatoes or bread on the side

- Pumpkin soup + potatoes or bread on the side

- Lentil soup + potatoes or bread on the side

- Potato soup with milk or soy milk + potatoes or bread on the side

- Chicken soup

- "Whatever's in the house" soup

[Other]

- Crockpot chicken supper
- Crockpot stew of vegetables
- Vegetarian chili
- Vegetable side dish: Frozen mixed veggies with fried onions and garlic, tomato paste, drop of brown sugar and lemon juice
- Rice with beans and salad
- Whole wheat couscous + chick peas + frozen corn with butter and salt (yummier than canned)
- Fried tofu strips with assorted vegetables on rice or with pita + corn chips
- Tofu spaghetti sauce over noodles (alternative to meat sauce)
- Hot dog and beans casserole + soup

Money Management Tips

Grocery Shopping—Stick to your list, don't shop when you're hungry, check sales, and then make your Shabbos menu, buy in bulk when your supermarket is running a good sale, and shop in stores with better prices even if they're less classy.

Quality—Sometimes more expensive, higher quality items save you money in the long run because they last much longer, such as, dish soap, sponges, stockings, small appliances, etc.

Snacks—Snacks are expensive and the supplies are depleted quickly. Baking is healthier and cheaper. Use reusable water bottles for sending drinks to school instead of box drinks.

Paper goods — There's always room to cut down on paper goods. Try one more meal a day using no paper goods. Try not using plastic cups at all except for guests. Alternatively, write each child's name on a plastic cup and use the same one the whole day. Use Pyrexes instead of disposable tins.

Make your own — Try out recipes for homemade ketchup, mayonnaise, marinara sauce, salad dressing, *techinah* and *chumus*. Make in bulk and freeze. Buy blocks of cheese and shred or slice it yourself, and freeze.

Water — Cut down on expensive drinks and juices by turning water back into the popular thirst-quenching drink it used to be. Buy funky straws and ice cube trays reserved just for drinks of water.

Clothing — Dare to buy one or two fewer items of clothing per person every season. Don't be taken in by every sale. Only go to a sale when you really need something. But only what you planned to buy.

Shoes — Try out stores like Target and Payless. You can get a few pairs for less than the price of one expensive pair.

Event guidelines — Stick to the guidelines set by your community's *Rabbanim* for *simchos* and *kiddushim*. Your community secretly appreciates it.

List of expenditures — Keep track of how much you spend on everything for one to two months. Make a list of how much you spent on groceries, vegetables, milk products, meat products, utilities, transportation, cleaning help, babysitting, prizes, pharmacy, take-out and miscellaneous. Beware of where all your money is going and see where you can cut down. Allot yourself a certain amount of money each month for extras and don't go over.

Chapter 7

Making Laundry Manageable

Chani's Laundry Wisdom

The folding challenge

Chani: As you probably have guessed, laundry is not exactly where I shine. I've come to terms with the realization that I've been avoiding this topic like I avoid my laundry! Actually, I'm very good about washing — I usually throw in a load or two every day. It's not the washing that's overwhelming — that, the machine does. It's the endless folding and putting away that bothers me. I take the clothes out of the dryer and dump them on a big table, out of sight, in the basement. I fold it if and when I can. My children know that when they can't find something to wear, they have to sift through the clothes on the basement table. My husband has been pushing me to hire someone just to fold the laundry and organize the closets, but I feel it's such a simple job, why waste the money?

Tova: It might be simple, but it's time consuming, boring and it's not getting done! If you would hire someone to do it, then the job would get done and you would feel on top of things.

Chani: We'll see. In the meanwhile, I do have some good tips that have really helped me with the ever present mountains of laundry.

Folding the clothing as is

For the time-consuming folding, I discovered that if I fold the clothing as is — without turning them outside in — then I really save time. It may be less convenient for the family members, but it's still better than leaving the laundry in a pile on the table.

Checking before throwing

I also taught my children to check their clothing to see if it needs washing before blindly throwing it into the hamper. I cut down on a lot of laundry that way.

Sarah: But even if you don't see the dirt, you never know what those clothes have come into contact with that day! Friends' runny noses, germs from busses and school bathrooms — anything!

Chani: Shhh! What I don't know doesn't bother me. Anyway, here's my last tip — and this one has cured the missing sock epidemic in my house. I hang a line with clothespins over the machine in the laundry room. Whenever I find a lonely sock, I hang it up on the line and eventually someone spots its pair. We've had some pretty exciting moments reuniting lost socks in my house. This works a lot better for me than being on the kids' backs to safety pin their socks together every night.

Clothesline for the single socks

Sarah: I know what you mean. I tried the safety pin routine, but only one of my children kept it up. So I came up with a different solution: I gave each child his or her own personal labeled mesh laundry bag for tights and socks. It's easier for them to put their socks in these than to pin them together. Sometimes, I have to remind the younger kids to put their socks into the mesh bags instead of into the hamper, but the older children remember on their own. They're motivated because they want their own socks back, not their sister's or brother's! When I do a wash, I throw the zipped mesh bags in. After the wash, I remove the tights and hang them to dry all in one spot, so that they stay together until they reach the drawers. I leave all the socks in and put the bags straight into the dryer. These mesh laundry bags are good for *tzitzis*, too.

Mesh sock bags

Dena: That would never work for me. I would forget to throw those bags in the wash if they weren't in the hamper. In my house every child has their own design on his or her socks that no other child has. That way I can

Different sock designs

immediately identify whose it is and find its pair. I have a friend that does just the opposite. She went out and bought all the girls the same design of tights/socks and all the boys exactly the same design, but in different sizes. She just matches sizes together and not designs.

Chani: Okay, well, I refuse to believe that none of you ever have missing socks once in a while, and I still think my sock line is revolutionary. But, enough about socks; let's get to our main topic. What kind of system do you use to manage the accumulation of dirty laundry? It's obviously a major part of a growing Jewish family's day-to-day life!

Dena's Daily Loads and Sorting Tips

Loading the machine at night

Dena: My system works pretty well for me. I'll tell you what I do. I keep three separate labeled hampers in the hall, centrally located between the bedrooms, for coloreds, whites and delicates. I chose nice wicker ones, since they're always in view. My children have learned to put their clothing into the correct hampers. Every night, one of the last things I do before I go to sleep is load up the washing machine with the contents of the fullest hamper. If necessary and if the fabric can handle it, I spray the clothing with a pretreat spray. The person who wakes up the earliest in the morning turns on the machine. Usually it's me, but often it's my husband on his way to *minyan*. A benefit of *vasikin*, I even have time to load up the dryer before I go off to work. Either way, I deal with the laundry at the first available moment when I come home.

Sorting while you hang

On hot days, I like to hang the laundry out to dry on the porch. I love having an excuse to get some sun.

Hanging the laundry doesn't take too much brain power, so I often use it as time to think and unwind. As I hang, I sort each child's clothing so that they hang together on the hanging rack. It keeps the clothing organized and makes for a much quicker folding process.

I installed shelves in the laundry room to hold every family member's personal clean laundry basket. As I remove the clothing from the dryer, I quickly sort all the clean laundry into the appropriate baskets. Every night, the laundry gets folded. It's not overwhelming at all, because it's just one load. If I can't get to it, I ask each capable child to fold and put away their own clothing. I have found that my children don't mind folding what belongs to them. It's folding the family's whole mountain of laundry that they have a problem with. If, for some reason, no one gets to the folding and putting away, at least it's sorted in the baskets or on the hanging rack, and everyone can find their things easily. If installing shelves doesn't work for you, there are stackable laundry baskets with front openings available in the home stores which serve the same purpose.

Personal clean laundry baskets

On my day off, I collect all the towels and do a towel wash. I also tie up all the loose ends — throwing in an extra load or two and putting away whatever articles of clothing are left in the baskets.

Sarah's Laundry Day and Ironing Tips

Sarah: I don't like doing the laundry daily. I find it monotonous and overwhelming to always have another load to do. I need the laundry to be finished at some point, even if it's only in my mind. So I created an end to laundry in my schedule.

I keep only one huge hamper in the main bathroom by the bedrooms. I tried the three separate hampers method, but my children never caught on, and I got frustrated finding loose items in the wrong hampers that already missed their turn in the wash. On Sunday night, I sit down with the hamper at my side, a big towel on my lap and four empty laundry baskets in front of me to sort whites, darks, lights and delicates. As I sort the week's laundry, I pretreat all the stains and scrub with a toothbrush when necessary. I use this time to catch up with a friend on the phone or to listen to an inspiring *shiur*.

I throw in a load or two on Sunday night, depending on how much time I have, and I lay the clean laundry from the dryer on an extra bed, where it waits to get folded. Monday is solely dedicated to laundry — washing, drying, folding and putting it away. I keep a needle and thread handy to quickly sew up small holes or missing buttons. It's an overwhelming sight, but I keep in mind that it's only one day and then I'm set for the week. I don't leave any major cooking or errands for Monday to make sure that I get the laundry done. I usually have some folding to do on Tuesday from my last loads of the day. After that, whatever is left, I leave as a chore for one of my older girls to do. By Tuesday night, I consider the laundry finished. I make sure to buy my family enough clothes to last an entire week.

Chani: Does anyone here iron or is that a task of the past?

Sarah: Actually, I happen to love ironing. I used to avoid it by putting the shirts in a hot dryer for a few minutes and then hanging them while they were still hot and wet. A good quality, wrinkle-free shirt is usually true to its name. As my older children became teenagers, they became more particular. So I parked myself in front of the ironing board armed with my spray starch and water spritzer, but it took an enormous amount of time! Sending all the clothes out to press was just too expensive, so I decided to do my research. Knowing that Europeans iron everything down to their undergarments, I asked a European acquaintance of mine what her secret was. She told me to get rid of my conventional steam iron and invest in a quality steam generator iron. I borrowed her iron for a day, so I could see for myself. The iron is attached to a water tank which boils the water; it shoots such powerful steam that the fabric becomes perfectly straight after just one swipe of the iron. After seeing such great results in so little time, I decided that it was a necessary investment if I wanted to successfully keep ironing in my schedule.

The other "must-do" is to keep the ironing board and iron open and available all the time. When my ironing board is neatly placed in the closet and the iron is high on a shelf, it is unlikely that I will get to it. I created a convenient spot in my basement to keep them accessible. Now I am able to perfectly iron any item of clothing in just seconds. My older children appreciate it and my husband enjoys his refined, polished look.

Tova's Ideas on Laundry

Tova: I'm very on top of the laundry although I never created a laundry schedule for myself. I keep a hamper in every bedroom, in order to increase the chances of the clothes making their way in there! I do the laundry whenever the hamper looks full. When a load is done, and I plan

Making sure to put away

to tend to it right away, I purposely dump it from the dryer onto the kitchen or dining room table to assure that I put it away before the next meal — or at least before my husband comes home.

Hanging rods in the laundry room

I have a few great tips for the laundry room that have changed my whole attitude towards laundry. There are many clothes that need to be hung to dry and I don't like hanging them on door knobs and in showers around the house. I installed a few rods in my laundry room just for this purpose. I have a towel rod on the wall and a tension pole in the doorway. I keep a basket of hangers handy and as soon as I pull something out of the washer/dryer that needs to be hung, I have a convenient place to hang it. In this way, I also avoid a lot of wasted time walking around the house looking for places to hang the clothes.

Sorting by size

I also sort the clean clothes in the laundry room, like you Dena, but slightly differently. I have a lot of boys close in age and they all wear clothing similar in style and size. I keep wire drawers in the laundry room which are labeled by size and not by name of child. The children are regularly growing out of their own size and into their older brother's size. When I fold undershirts, shirts and pants, I put it in the drawer marked with the appropriate size. At some point I put it away, but in the meantime, it's folded and sorted so that a child who has run out of clean clothes can grab something that's his size or close to it.

Multitasking

I like to multitask when I'm folding or putting away the laundry. I don't have a set time for doing it, but as soon as I get a phone call, I head towards the laundry room. Phone headsets are great for this purpose. Alternatively, I use folding time to bond with a child.

I try not to let the large amounts of laundry get to me. It helps me when I remind myself how thankful I am to have so many special people who need their clothes washed and how grateful I am to own all the clothes that they need.

Maintaining a positive attitude

Stain Removal Tips
(check on hidden part of clothing first)

- Use hot water if clothing can handle it, and a good detergent. Cheaper detergents do not do as good a job.

- Don't overload the washing machine.

- Use a toothbrush to scrub out stains with soap or spray.

- Use a good quality stain spray or stick.

- Presoak stains in a bucket with detergent and spray in advance.

- When you notice a stain, treat it and soak it as soon as possible.

- Bleach stains out with a Q-tip dipped in bleach or with a bleach pen (whites only!).

- Use rubbing alcohol as an alternative to bleach.

- Use quality dish soap or baby powder to pretreat oily stains.

- Try hair spray, acetone or seltzer on all kinds of stains.

- Rub milk into water-based stains.

- Hours of strong sunlight helps to bleach out a stain.

- Bibs: Try buying decorative big towel bibs to protect children's clothing. You might be surprised to find that even older children are willing to wear them to avoid dirtying a favorite shirt.

Chapter 8

Bored Children

The Root of Boredom

Dena: If there is one thing that gets to me it's when my kids are bored! So much of their free time is taken up with activities we do together or which require my input — like playing, *shmoozing*, mealtime, driving them where they want to go — that when it comes to the rest of their free time, I wish they would just figure out what to do on their own. I dread the days when there's no school. Is the ability to entertain themselves something I can teach them?

Tova: I also had a period of time where my kids were constantly complaining of boredom. I tried to analyze the situation and find the cause of the problem. Was there something I could change that would make a difference? Could it be that we didn't have enough toys? Was there some issue of dynamics between the children? I came up with three main causes of boredom. Understanding why they were bored helped me to cut down on the frequency of the complaining in my house.

Lack of a structured schedule   Any time there was a lack of structure in their day, they were bored — *erev* Shabbos, Shabbos, Sunday, Yom Tov and other vacation days. I realized that when a child approached me in that whiney voice and said, "Mommeeee... I don't have anything to do! I'm bored!" they were really asking for structure. So I started making schedules for my family for those unstructured days. I included the daily routines, as well as new ideas for activities. I added some simple pictures and hung it on the fridge. The kids began to look forward to these schedules. They were excited to keep to the program, and didn't even notice that no special activity was actually going on!

A "boring" vacation day, with nothing in particular planned might get a schedule like this:

Wake up, morning routine, get dressed
9:00:   Start *davening*
9:45:   Eat sandwiches
10:00:   Build skyscrapers out of all the building toys! See how tall you can build them.
11:15:   Cleanup time
11:30:   Arts and Crafts with "surprise supplies" (new glitter glue or something to make the usual more interesting)
12:30:   Cleanup
1:00:   Lunch — Pancakes
1:40:   Go to the local park with snacks
4:00:   Plan a puppet show for Shira's birthday party this Shabbos
5:15:   Practice performance for Mommy
6:00:   Dinner
6:45:   Baths, reading time, bedtime begins

Of course, it's hard to keep exactly to the times listed, but the schedule is a good guideline for how the day should progress. If I would try to suggest to the kids to do the same activities without an official schedule, I would probably hear, "I'm not in the mood," and "I don't want to!" For some reason, this way, the children are happy to follow instructions, and they're busy, not bored.

I also found that boredom is sometimes a result of my demeanor in the house. When the kids sense that I'm focused on my own thing, or notice that I'm edgy about something, they pick up on it and feel unsettled. It may result in

Reacting to Mommy's mood

"I'm bored!" but really they are saying, "What's the matter, Mommy? Something doesn't feel right." When I'm aware that I'm feeling this way, I try to preempt the restlessness with an activity before they even notice my edginess.

Calling for attention

Another common source for the bored complaint is a justified need for attention. Sometimes, just *shmoozing* with a child a bit or reading him a short book is all that's necessary to get him to snap out of it. An investment of ten to fifteen minutes can sometimes yield an hour's worth of the child playing on his own!

Needing an outlet for creativity

Sarah: I'll give you a fourth cause of boredom. My kids get bored a lot because my house is too structured. Allowing my children to be creative and self-sufficient usually means a big mess, and you know me, I avoid that as much as possible. Arts and crafts means sticky glue, little scraps of paper, drops of paint and splattered glitter. Baking means a kitchen full of flour and dough. A skyscraper with all the building toys in the house is a big cleanup job which no child will take on. When my son practices his drums, it's so noisy that I grit my teeth until he's finished.

I am working on keeping a proper balance between being clean and organized, yet still allowing my children to foster their creativity and talents. It's really hard for me, but I hope to figure it out one day soon. I try to keep in mind your motto, Tova: "A home has to be clean enough to be healthy, but messy enough to be happy." Of course my children are often bored — I'm never in the mood to let them do anything!

Deciding if it's worth it

Tova: Sarah, I can give you two pieces of advice that will work well with your personality. First, whenever one of my kids comes up with an interesting idea for an activity,

I ask myself, "For how long will this activity keep them occupied? Will the mess it will make be worth it?" Some examples are: a tent with all the pillows and blankets in the house, a project with paper-mache, or a water fight. Sometimes, the valuable peaceful time I'm gaining is really worth the mess! If it's not worth it, I'll say no.

I also ask myself, "Is the skill my child will gain from this activity a worthwhile investment?" My daughter asked me if she could bake challah for the first time after I had just cleaned up the kitchen. She's never in the mood to bake and I really wanted her to learn to make challah. I agreed because she was inspired to do it, even though it wasn't good timing for me. That's probably why you put up with your son's drum lessons. You realize that it's good for him even though you can't stand the noise.

My second idea for you is right up your alley. A great way to teach kids to be independent and to entertain themselves is by keeping their activities available and accessible. Here's what I did: I set up an arts and crafts area in the kitchen that holds everything they need for a wide range of projects. All the supplies are easily accessible so that the kids can find things by themselves. I showed them how to keep it organized, set the rules, and put a kiddie table in the kitchen. Whenever they like, they are allowed to do whatever creative art project that they want. As long as they clean up after themselves, they're entitled to this privilege.

Keeping supplies accessible

In my house, this area is in the kitchen, because I like to be available to help them, but you can do this in the playroom if that works better for you. I cleared out space under the kitchen sink where I put assorted labeled containers: one container with white glue, glue sticks, scissors, staplers and tape, a second container with colorful stickers and another with washable water paint, and a few smaller containers with a variety of interesting materials — pompoms, popsicle sticks, sequins, pieces of shinny wrapping paper, etc. I keep a small pile of workbooks and nice coloring books in there, too. On the inside of the cabinet door, I attached a manila envelope to hold coloring paper, tracing paper and construction paper. And most basic, I keep a divided tray of crayons, markers, colored pencils and oil pastels in the cabinet, too.

Surprise basket

The exciting feature of this cabinet is the "surprise basket." Every once in a while, especially before an upcoming vacation day, I'll add a new craft supply to the basket like modeling clay, googly eyes, pipe cleaners or tissue paper. Having something new to work with, especially when it's a surprise, really adds excitement and keeps the kids interested!

Other outlets for creativity

You can do the same sort of thing with baking supplies for the older girls or construction materials for the older boys. A hammer, nails and scraps of wood can keep a boy entertained for hours! Set it up properly and teach him how to maintain it, and you won't have a mess. A child who is always dependent on Mommy for ideas and permission for each and every activity will be less likely to entertain himself, while a child who has activities and materials available to him can be tremendously creative and keep himself very busy.

I think this "activity cabinet" idea can really work for you because it's an organized way to teach children self-sufficiency.

Accepting boredom

Dena: I still think that there is just nothing to do sometimes! The child is simply in "bored mode" and you can't get him out of it. Not a suggestion in the world will help. It's annoying, but I've learned that I can't fix everything and it's okay if the kids are bored at times. It doesn't mean that I'm a bad mother.

Tova: It's true. You're a hundred percent right; sometimes a child is just inconsolably bored. When my kids get like that, I just try to empathize with them until they find something to do. Often the children just need to get out, especially boys. Letting out their energy on bicycles or in the park can give them stamina to play nicely at home afterwards.

Sarah: The hardest situation for me used to be when a child would be home sick. I'm busy with my morning routine and I can't sit and play games all morning. So I invested in two special games that can be played by one person alone, and I save them solely for sick days. It completely solved the problem! *Sick days*

To help avoid general boredom, I make a real effort to encourage reading in my children from a young age. Reading can keep them busy for hours! And of course, it's also so good for their development. I keep a large supply of age-appropriate books at home; we buy, borrow and share, so there's always something for everyone. *Books*

Chani: I find that keeping up with the seasonal changes in hobbies helps keep the kids busy with their friends. During sticker trading season, I make sure my children are well-stocked with stickers to trade. At the first sight of spring, I'm the first to buy my girls new jump ropes and Chinese jump ropes. *Kugelach* and Rebbe/mitzvah card trading are always in season. For considerably low cost, my kids are equipped to be entertained for hours on end. *Encouraging hobbies*

Dena: You've all offered some really great ideas about coping with children's boredom, but I still feel like I can use some practical suggestions for activities for kids who are tired of all their toys.

Tova: You can try the bookstore or library for activity and crafts books. There are some really good creative books out there. And I'll be happy to share my own list of activities that work well for my family. I also wrote up a list of original things to do with just paper, which is really useful when you don't have any special supplies in the house.

Popular Activities in Tova's House

Dress up — Use old Purim costumes, hats, handbags and aprons for acting out story tapes, playing make-believe and performing shows.

White board art — Keep a large board with an assortment of colored markers for playing school, tic-tac-toe or just plain coloring.

Play-doh — Invest in good Play-doh toys.

Tunnels and tents — These are great for making an obstacle course or playhouse.

Arts and crafts — Keep a nice assortment of supplies and replenish as needed.

Make believe store — Allow the kids to use real canned and packaged foods to make a store. Give them a table to "set up shop" and shopping bags for "customers." Alternatively, they can use all the shoes in the house, or some of the toys.

Real store — Have the kids set up a "real" store by buying food products to prepare and sell, such as ice cream, baked goods or sandwiches. This is a two day activity — one day to prepare, and one day to sell. Have them invite friends and family to come and buy their favorite foods.

Family slumber party — Use sleeping bags to camp out in the living room. Treat everyone to late night snacks, a family game and stories with flashlights.

Colored water — Cut off the top half of some empty plastic soda bottles to make funnels for water play. Fill up a few soda bottles with water and food colorings. Kids love to pour the water and mix and match colors.

Shaving cream — 1) Fill up a big cookie sheet with shaving or whip cream. Have kids drive toy cars through it and make roads and highways. 2) Balloon shaving contest.

Hairdo day — Do everyone's hair up fancy, invite friends over and have a mock *simchah*.

Toilet paper contest — This is an activity for four children or more. Divide the children into two or more groups of two. See which pair can wrap each other in toilet paper first.

Freeze dance — Follow the leader to music.

Scavenger hunt in the supermarket — Make up an assignment, such as, to find the items whose names begin with the letters of a particular word. For example, for the word "Sunday," they may find spaghetti, umbrella, nuts, deli, apples, and yogurt.

Scavenger hunt around the neighborhood — Place clues

by neighbors and friendly local stores. The last clue leads to a prize.

Bean hunt in a grassy park — Scatter a large amount of beans (or something more exciting, like small wrapped candies) in a large area of the park. Give everyone a bag. Whoever collects the most wins a prize (or the candies he or she collected).

Park challenges — Challenge kids to slide down the playground slide holding a cup of water without spilling.

Tova's Paper Projects

Decorate the house — Have the children make a big paper chain string and hang it across the ceiling. Hang everyone's Yom Tov or birthday related pictures from it, using string and a hole puncher.

Coloring — Trace a child's body on very large pieces of oak tag (or two stuck together). Kids can draw their features and clothing and color themselves in.

Murals — Line a bedroom wall with large sheets of coloring paper and allow the kids to "color on the wall."

Dollhouse — Make a doll house and furniture out of cardboard boxes, shoe boxes, match boxes, medicine boxes and any other type of cardboard you have in the house.

Dolls — Cut simple paper dolls out of cereal boxes and design clothing out of construction paper to slide over the doll's head (cut slit down back of dress).

Games — Design your own board game or card game with

the kids, such as, Chutes and Ladders, Twister, Candy Land, or a matching game. You can illustrate it with pictures from a magazine of an upcoming holiday. Laminate for long-term use.

Paper creations — Origami, paper airplanes.

Scavenger hunt in newspaper/magazine — Make a list of items to look for, cut out and paste onto construction paper (house with furniture, table with food, store with clothes, etc.).

Mosaic — Cut small squares out of a magazine and divide the pieces into different piles of colors. Make a beautiful mosaic with all the squares of colors (seven species, rainbow, house with grass and trees, etc.).

Surprise package — Put a hidden prize under many layers of wrapped newspaper. On every layer, write a riddle or instructions for a funny task. Play music and pass the package around in a circle. When the music stops, the person holding the package unwraps one layer and does what the note says. The prize should be something everyone can enjoy such as, balloons, lollipops or stickers.

Paper-mache — Cut strips of newspaper and dip in a mixture of one part flour and three parts water. Wrap the layers around a balloon, toilet paper rolls or yogurt containers, to create a form. Paint when dry.

Decorative cylinders — Keep folding each individual page of a magazine in half into the center a few times. Do this with every page in the magazine until you have a solid cylinder. This can be used with other cylinders to hang as a mobile or *sukkah* decoration or as a building block for another project. You can weave them together to make a basket or a box.

Family picture — Sit in a circle. One child starts drawing a picture. Another repeatedly rolls a die. When a six comes up, the paper and pen is passed to the next player to continue drawing the same picture.

Spring —
Adar, Nisan, Iyar

Chapter 9
Organizing the Home – I

Maximizing Space in the Kitchen

Center of family activities

Sarah: The kitchen is definitely the most important room in my house. Of course, its most basic function is a place to prepare all the food and serve all our meals. But beyond that, it's the center of family activities and bonding experiences. As our family grew, I found it difficult to maintain such an active kitchen—serving three meals a day plus snacks, hosting homework sessions, occasional arts and crafts projects (yes, even I do those once in a while!) and late night *shmoozing* over snacks and drinks.

Getting rid of unusable items

I really don't do well amid chaos, so I felt that I needed to minimize the clutter in my kitchen and organize our things in a way that could be easily maintained.

So I picked a day to focus on making the kitchen more functional. No more, "One day I'll get to that." I finally committed. Today was the day! First I opened up all the cabinets to see what I had. I took out all the broken pots and rusty utensils that were filling up precious space. Anything broken that I could fix, I kept and fixed right then and there, anything that I couldn't fix, I tossed. Then I began reorganizing my cabinets.

Smaller stacks in upper cabinets

It wasn't too hard to uncover problem number one. I had too many dishes stacked one on top of the other. My meat set of twelve, which consisted of dishes, bowls and appetizer plates, were all crammed into one shelf. When I needed a dish for a quick snack, it was a whole ordeal to pry it out. I calculated that I only needed six of everything on a regular basis, so I removed the rest. I was then able to put every dish and bowl in a neat separate pile.

My dairy cabinet is smaller, so in order to store the different size plates separately, I needed to maximize the storage space. I measured and figured out what size wire shelving I needed to make it work, and scheduled a time to shop for them.

Now that I had my upper cabinets all figured out, I was left with a counter full of all the extra dishes I had taken out! I noticed that I had a lot of dead space in all my upper cabinets, so I readjusted the notches of my shelves and added more brackets to create another shelf. I put all my extra dishes on the top shelf. When I saw how easy it was to make use of that extra space, I decided it was time to head over to the hardware store. I bought more brackets and shelves and maximized the space in every cabinet in the house! By the time I was finished, I was able to cross the island off my dream kitchen wish list; I didn't need the space anymore!

Adding extra shelves

Next were the lower cabinets and drawers. First, I removed all the things I hardly used: Bubby's melon baller, the fancy vegetable cutter that I use only on Tu B'Shevat, cookie cutters that I'm supposed to use when I bond with my children, a long set of skewers that I never used to grill vegetables, and a hand grater that I keep just in case my food processor would be out of commission. Up they went, in a basket, on one of my new shelves. Since I use these utensils only a few times a year, I felt it was more practical to move them to a top shelf and clear up space where I need it the most.

Making space in lower cabinets

I had to decide which drawers were essential for daily use. In those drawers, I put what I use all the time and nothing more: my silverware, knives, basic pots, and colander. I maximized the space in the drawers by dividing the smaller ones with baskets to keep small items organized, and the larger ones lengthwise with a divider.

Keeping essentials in drawers

Containers   The biggest waste of space was my drawer of containers. I had containers of every size and shape in there. I took stock and realized that I never used the containers that didn't stack well in the refrigerator. It was time to get rid of them; they weren't worth an entire drawer of prime space in my kitchen. Out they went, and I had an entire extra drawer to play with! I replaced all those random-shaped containers with a neat set of rectangular ones — three sizes with varying depths — that take up a quarter of the space in my drawer. They all stack into one neat pile, and all the covers fit all the containers, so I never have to go fishing!

Paper goods center   Next was my paper goods center. This had to be planned well, since this drawer gets constant usage, all day long. I removed all the loose open packages and made separate neat piles of big plates, small plates, bowls and cups. I put two baskets in the drawer — one for forks and one for spoons. I kept one closed extra package of each item in the drawer and the rest I stored high up on a shelf to take down when I run out. Now I had an accessible, functional paper goods center.

Cup dispenser   **Chani:** I'm glad to hear that even you have to reorganize every now and then, Sarah! And the best part is that your ideas don't seem too difficult to apply. I must add that I found a plastic cup dispenser to be the ideal solution for storing those tall stacks of cups while still making them accessible.

Separating pots from lids   I also want to mention the advantage of storing pot lids separately from the pots. Ever since I separated them, I'm always able to find the pot and lid that I need right away.

Sarah: Those are great ideas! My kitchen is still in the process of reorganization, so I need as many good ideas as I can get.

Tova: Well then, I must share with you some things I've read on kitchen organization that have absolutely changed my life. These ideas come from *Confessions of an Organized Homemaker* by Deniece Schofield (Betterway Books, 1994, Cincinnati, Ohio). Maybe they will help you. First, when deciding where to keep certain items in your kitchen, be aware of how many motions it takes to reach the item when you need it. The simpler it is to reach something you need, the more functional you are and the more likely that cabinet will stay neat. Items that you use a few times a day should take only one to two motions. I put things like ketchup, peanut butter and coffee within easy reach and not behind pantry items that I use only once a week. I store the electric sandwich maker and the pasta strainer, both of which I use four to five times a week, in a more accessible place than my once-a-week *cholent* pot or hot water urn. This analysis really enhances efficiency in the kitchen.

Becoming "motion-minded"

The next idea that I incorporated is not a traditional one, yet extremely practical. I choose where to store kitchen products based on their use in the kitchen rather than with similar items. For example, baking supplies and ingredients are typically spread throughout the kitchen — the baking paper is with the paper goods, the vanilla and chips are in the pantry, the mixer is with the small appliances and the mixing bowl is with the pots or the dishes. With such a set up, by the time you finish baking a cake, you've wasted time walking around the kitchen five or six times! After reading about this idea, I took a

Storing according to use

basket and put all of my baking items in it — the hand mixer, vanilla, chips, sprinkles, cocoa, baking soda, baking powder, etc. For products that I don't only use for baking, it is worth buying two of the same — one to store in my baking basket and one to keep in the pantry. Since I bake often, I keep my baking basket in a cabinet right above the workspace on the counter where I keep my mixing bowl.

My sister did the same with her salad accessories. She stores her cutting board, vegetable peeler, knife, salad spinner and bowl all on the same shelf. She claims she's apt to make a salad more easily because she has set it up so conveniently.

I keep my sandwich bags with my dairy silverware and not with my paper goods because when I'm making sandwiches, I'm always standing near that drawer. I keep my paper goods in a cabinet near the kitchen table because that's where we use them. Pots go in a cabinet near the stove top. I have a cabinet over the main part of my dairy counter where I keep all the different items that I use all day long — bread, peanut butter, rice cakes, baby cereal, coffee, vitamins, chocolate milk powder and the sandwich grill.

Sarah: What creative ideas! Tova, do you think you could come over and help me think through how to redo a few more of my cabinets?

Tova: I would love to, but I'm warning you: This new approach had me coming up with some very unconventional places to keep things. I'm not sure you could handle it, Sarah!

Reevaluating
regularly

Sarah: You're probably right, but it's always helpful to hear new ideas. I'm constantly reevaluating how I've set up my home. My needs and my family's needs are always changing, so I find that I need to redo cabinets and shelves on a regular basis. For example, one of my daughters is into dieting right now, so salads have recently been taking over my kitchen. Another is into sewing, so I have to find a place for her new hobby. Now my husband started learning at home in the evening, so we've set up a makeshift study in the guest room. Even if some of your interesting ideas won't work for me now, I'll hold on to them for future reference.

Dena, you've been so quiet. Can you let us in on your secrets of how you run such a smooth operation in your kitchen?

Dena: My ideas will only help you if you plan on redoing your kitchen. I spent a lot of time planning the design of my kitchen before I had it done. I looked at a lot of different kitchens, and I spoke to many carpenters to get cabinetry ideas. I came up with some great innovative designs. For example, I have a tall and narrow cabinet designed just to hold my hot plate and some big baking trays. I chose a sink that came with a special cutting board that snaps right onto it. This gives me extra counter space and comes in handy to hide my dirty dishes when I don't have time to wash them. Another nice feature that I have in my kitchen is a small drawer that slides from right to left inside my cutlery drawers, on top of the silverware. I keep my serving utensils in there so that they don't get mixed in with the silverware. I also built a narrow closet that is just the right size for my mop, broom and dust pan. I have a small rectangular shelf that I use to keep the bread just above my counter. There are so many different ideas out there! When I did my research, I was always second-guessing myself and thinking that maybe I was overdoing it. But, I'm happy to

Designing according to needs

say that I created a very functional and efficient kitchen that satisfies all my needs. My money was well-spent.

Replacing bags with containers

Chani: You are all so creative and fancy! I can offer the basics. I keep containers for many items in my pantry to keep it clean and organized, so that partially opened bags of nosh, cereal and pasta don't make a mess. I also have a box of clothespins and twist-ties handy in my cutlery drawer to close any open bag that doesn't have a container. I avoid many messes this way.

Finding a "home" in the refrigerator

No one has mentioned the refrigerator. When my refrigerator and freezer turned into a state of emergency, I took everything out, scrubbed it down and then called Tova. She helped me create a home for everything in my fridge. Now, condiments are always on the door, cheeses are always in the drawer, meat containers are on one side and dairy on the other. I keep my spices on a small shelf on the door and, as Tova instructed, I even labeled the tops of the canisters so that I can find the one I need without having to shuffle through all of them. Believe me, this wasn't easy for me, but it was well worth pushing myself! Also, before I put in all the fresh Shabbos food on Friday, I give the fridge a quick once over to make sure no old leftovers or empty bottles or containers are lurking anywhere. My refrigerator has so much more space now. Having a clean and functional fridge turned out to be key for me in the smooth running of my kitchen.

Sarah: Chani, that's exactly what I do in my refrigerator! I just took it one step further and labeled all the shelves so that my family members know where to put things back. There is no more rummaging through the fridge in my house; I can find what I'm looking for right away.

Now that we've got all the food-related stuff in the kitchen figured out, I want to point out that there is so much more that comes in and out of the kitchen than groceries, pots and dishes. When I realized that my kitchen counter was everyone's favorite spot for everything, I knew it was time to find a place for each and every item that would get left there. Car keys, house keys, papers, pens, drinking cups, vitamins, paper towel rolls and everything in between. It wasn't that my family was messy, it was just that everything needed a designated place. I asked some friends for ideas, and then I shopped around in houseware stores, and this is what I came up with.

Dealing with clutter on counters

I attached a long shelf to the bottom of my upper cabinets. On that shelf I put a few pretty baskets — one long one for pens, pencils and a pair of scissors, one basket for house, car and bicycle keys, one basket for daily vitamins and medicines and one catch-all basket for odds and ends. I also made room to put a stapler, scotch tape dispenser and a sticky memo pad on that shelf. If I had the room, I would also put an electric pencil sharpener there. In addition I attached a paper towel holder under another section of cabinets. I created "a place for everything" and I put "everything in its place." My counters really stay clutter-free. I'm telling you, this really works.

Shelf under upper cabinets

Tova: Now all you have to do is to train your family to put their things in the appropriate basket instead of on the counter. Good luck!

Sarah: Yeah, it took a while, but, little by little they caught on. Although they won't admit it, my family also appreciates a functional home. They enjoy being able to find something when they need it.

Ever present
drinking cups

Dena: What do you do about all the drinking cups? I either have cups all over the counter or we go through a sleeve of cups in a day. What a mess and what a waste!

Sarah: There are lots of great ideas to solve that one. A friend of mine keeps a tray on her counter with a pitcher of water and a cup for every member of the family. After they take a drink, they rinse the cup and put it right back on the tray—no buildup of cups in the sink or on the counter. I've also seen a "cup tree" sold in stores. It's similar to a coat stand, but obviously smaller and it takes up less counter space than a tray. I came up with my own idea. I installed seven hooks, evenly spaced, under the shelf which I installed under my upper cabinets, where I hung seven coordinated plastic mugs. After someone takes a drink, he or she rinses the mug and puts it back on the hook instead of cluttering the counter. Alternatively, you can attach the hooks directly to the underside of the cabinet itself.

Chani: Do they really put them back?

Sarah (laughing): Not necessarily, but I still enjoy that everything that lands on my counter has a home. It makes it easy for me to quickly make space on my counter when I'm about to cook or serve a meal.

Dena: Does every family member have their own cup?

Color coding **Sarah:** No, we all share. But, I have an idea for the future, which might be over the top, even for me. Listen to this: Every family member chooses a color, and all their things are labeled in that color, such as their drinking cup, toothbrush, sock bag, books—you can go as far as you want with this. In this way, all ages can quickly identify anything that is theirs. It would make it easy for me or any other able hands to put away everyone's laundry and belongings. I think things could run really smoothly using this system, but I think my family would have my head.

Dena: It sounds like my office!

Sarah: Offices run smoothly because large operations have to be extremely organized to be productive. Really, I don't see why a large family should be any different.

Chani: That is profound, Sarah!

Organizing the Toys

Sarah: When I see toys lying around my house, even in the playroom, it makes me nervous. My boys have loads of construction toys, the older girls have stacks of board games, and I think the little girls have more dolls and kitchen accessories than Toys 'R Us! Of course, I know that all these toys are here to stay; they're important for the kids' development and they're a big part of our life for now. So in order to keep my sanity, I had to organize the toys in such a way that it looked neat and would be easy for the kids to maintain.

I used a toy chest when the kids were younger, but as they grew and their toy needs became more involved, I realized it was time for a new solution. I took a trip to the housewares store — the owner is really fond of me by now! — where I bought uniform clear plastic containers for all of our toys. When we get a new toy, I take everything out of the original box and put it all in the right sized container. Lego, blocks and bigger building toys go in large containers; puzzles, toys with pieces and play dishes go in

Uniform containers

medium ones; and games with small pieces go in the little ones. I bought an inexpensive shelving unit that stores everything beautifully. There are lots of different shelving options out there to choose from to suit a variety of tastes and budgets. The key is that everything is uniform. Rectangular containers stack better than circular ones, and they keep the shelves organized and neat. My sister does the same thing with baskets.

Wall and ceiling space   I also have a net hanging from the ceiling of the playroom to hold dolls and stuffed animals in the corner of the room. We installed sturdy hooks on the wall to hold bicycles, our trampoline, doll carriages and other large items that just clutter the room if they don't have a storage place.

Reinforcing boxes and binding books   **Tova:**   I actually like keeping most things in their original boxes. To me, toys look more appealing and exciting that way. I keep games neatly stacked on open shelves in the playroom so that the kids can see what they have. As soon as we get a new game, I reinforce the box with strong tape to make them sturdier. Eventually, if the box falls apart, I switch to a container. I reinforce books too. I don't bind them properly, although that's a good idea, but I cover them with a plastic book cover and cover the spine and the inside of the cover with tape.

Plastic set of drawers   For toys, I use plastic drawers. They keep the toys accessible and easy to put away. I have a few different sets in different sizes in the playroom. In one set, each drawer has a different building toy. In another set, I store the cars, play dishes, puzzles and Playmobil, and the third set has small dolls, doll clothing, doll furniture and little people.

I think these drawers are so practical that I even have

a set of them in the corner of my living room. Each drawer is labeled with a different child's name. When I find the kids' belongings lying around the house, I put it in their drawer. The kids are expected to clean out their drawers every few days. This way, they don't lose their stuff, it's not in my way, and everybody's happy.

Dena: I do something similar to that, Tova. I keep a collection basket of misplaced things. When I only have a few minutes to straighten up, I collect everything that's not in its place and put it into this basket. When I get around to it, I distribute the toy parts, game pieces, school supplies and whatnot to their proper places. The basket is also very useful to my cleaning help; she puts everything she finds in there, and I can feel confident that important game pieces are not getting thrown out.

Collection basket

Sarah, I also do something similar to your upper kitchen cabinet system with my toys. I noticed that I had many unused toys cluttering up my shelves. There were puzzles, Lotto games, old card games, travel games and cheap games from the dollar store. I took them out of their packaging and put them each in a Ziploc bag which I then placed in a box on a high shelf. That gave me more room for the toys that the kids play with on a regular basis. Now, I pull this box down when we need toys to take on trips or when I need to bring out something new for a change. These unused toys actually became our most exciting toys.

Box of unused toys

Chani: I must confess that I still use a toy chest. I find it very convenient for quick cleanups. Once every two to three months, I make an activity of cleaning out the toy chest with my kids. We put all the toy and game pieces

Making a toy chest work

back in their containers and boxes, and we throw out the broken toys or those with too many missing pieces. It's actually a very good activity, and it helps get the kids interested in their toys once again.

Kid's projects and artwork

Dena: Another thing I do to minimize clutter in the playroom—and this is a real twenty-first century solution—is scan all my kids' projects into the computer and then throw them in the garbage. Not right away, of course, only when the kids are tired of them. I know it sounds cold, but there is a limit to how many projects that I can keep laying around the house. A friend of mine took this idea even further and printed out the pictures of her kids' projects and put them in a nice album that the kids look at from time to time. It's actually a nice way to save all the memories without buying a new cabinet.

Sarah: Maybe I'll try that one day. The first thing I do when a child brings home a drawing is hang it on the giant corkboard in the playroom. I rotate the artwork regularly, and the most special ones get saved in large envelopes—separate ones for each child. I co-opt the kids in this and let them choose which they want to save. One thing's for sure, though: Their artwork and projects don't find their way into the bedrooms, or their bedrooms would turn into playrooms!

Bedroom Space

Tova: Thanks, Sarah. That brings us right into our next topic! I have a lot of great ideas for maximizing bedroom space. I have four girls in one small bedroom, and there's space for a desk and a play area in there, too.

Sarah: Please do tell!

Tova: We bought a bunk bed with two slide-out beds underneath. It's four beds in the space of one! Though I must admit, it took us a long time to feel comfortable with this purchase. *Pull-out bunk beds*

Sarah: Why?

Tova: Well, we actually owned enough beds for all our children, but we didn't have the space in the house to comfortably put them all.

Sarah: So you invested in a quadruple bed set in order to maximize space.

Tova: Exactly. We sold our old beds through a second hand furniture dealer. In retrospect, I am really happy with our decision. It was much more affordable than moving or extending our house, and we really gained some more space. We also installed two nice-sized fold-down desks onto the wall next to the beds, and the children use these to do their homework. During the day, with the beds tucked away and the desks folded, we have a big play area. An added bonus is that there is no accumulation of clutter in the room because there is no surface to dump things on. We keep two folding chairs in the corner of the room and we have shelves above the desks for the kids' books and supplies.

Dena: My kids would never go for a bunk bed!

Tova: There are all kinds of pull-out beds available, not just bunk beds. The store I shopped in also had a bed that's slightly higher than standard height with three beds that pulled out from underneath. Your house is about the same size as mine. How do you fit everyone into your bedrooms?

Dena: I don't know if this will be helpful or not, but like with my kitchen, I had a carpenter design the kids' bedrooms. He came up with all sorts of unique designs to accommodate all of our needs. Desks, beds, drawers, closets —he fit everything in. I did spend a lot more money, but I tried to rationalize it as a big saving since I didn't need to move or expand my apartment.

Tova: I'd like your carpenter's phone number. I have another bunk bed in the boy's room. I think I can probably have a pull-out bed built to fit under it, too.

Chani: Tova, what do you do about closet space for four children in one room?

Tova: When we added the fourth child in the girl's room, I was afraid that we would have to keep her clothing somewhere else. My husband figured out a way to make more room by taking out the top shelf in the closet and adding another hanging rod. Now there is room for two rods of hanging clothes in the closet—a higher one and a lower one. My older daughters hang their clothes on the upper rod with the help of a step stool and the younger girls share the bottom rod. Another way to do it would be to keep the four girls' weekday shirts and skirts on the bottom rod and use the upper rod for Shabbos and afternoon clothes.

You know, I've seen homes where the children's bedrooms have no closets whatsoever. Instead, one bedroom down the hall is designed as a walk-in closet for all the children to share. This enables the children to have plenty of play space in their rooms, as well as comfortable closet space.

In order to keep the clutter in the bedrooms to a minimum, I put a set of plastic drawers in each bedroom for everyone's "treasures." Everyone gets a drawer and saves as many things as fit in there. Every now and then, they clean out their drawers to make room for their new "treasures." It's interesting to see how they decide what to keep and what to throw away.

Chani: You know, I had such a problem with closet space in the kids' rooms that I ran a yard sale and simply got rid of a lot of their clothing. I kept exactly what was needed — four to six weekday outfits, two Shabbos outfits and one to two pairs of pajamas for each child. I only store hand-me-downs that are in excellent condition and I give away the rest. Without having all the extras around, I minimize laundry buildup and I'm able to keep the closets much neater.

Keeping only what's needed

Tova: You don't keep any extra clothes? If something is on sale, you wouldn't just buy it, just in case?

Chani: It is really tempting to buy sale items, but I try really hard not to. I don't enjoy reorganizing my closets, so my best solution is to keep as little as I can in them.

Sarah: So my storage containers would probably frighten you. I bought eight of the largest transparent storage containers, and I store clothes sorted and labeled by age (not by season and not by gender). When one of the children grows into the next size, I put all his clothing back into the box it came from, regardless of the season. I keep all the boxes easily accessible all of the time. I know someone who even keeps them nicely stacked in the corner of the bedroom. If I feel that the closets are overstuffed or if I see that a child doesn't like some of his or her outfits, I simply return them to the correct box. I don't have to wait for the next season when we "take down the boxes." I don't have

Storing hand-me-downs

a million, different, little boxes separating each type of clothing. For example, Shabbos dresses, age 3, summer; boys, age 5, winter sweaters, etc. It's too confusing and it just doesn't work for me.

I try to minimize what I save, but even so, I do save a lot of extras. You never know what the next child is going to like and I don't like spending money if I don't have to. Here's a good tip, though: I have found that when the children reach adolescence, it's almost pointless to save hand-me-downs for them. By the time they get to it, it is out of style, so it doesn't pay to waste the space saving it. Containers cost money too; just ask my husband, he'll tell you!

Making use of hooks   Another thing I do to contain the clutter is hang hooks. I have hooks everywhere — heavy metal ones that hang over the door, hooks in the bedrooms for sock bags, hooks in the bathroom and in the front hall. I try to create a place for everything that might be lying around the house, robes, sweaters, pocketbooks, hats, wallets, towels, etc. The problem now is that the clutter is hanging on the wall. At least it's off the floor. Every once in a while, I sort through all the things on the hooks, put them away, and then the house is clutter-free again.

Chapter 10

Organizing the Home – II

Traffic Center

Tova: As soon as the kids walk in from school, they dump their knapsacks, sweaters, shoes, books and lunch boxes right in the front hall. And in the winter, there are coats, umbrellas and boots, too! Then when my husband comes home, he adds his *tallis* bag, briefcase, *sefarim*, wallet, keys and hat. Where do you all keep these things? Near the front door? In the bedrooms? I need some sort of system to control all the incoming and outgoing stuff. HELP!

Front hall closet **Dena:** We keep everything except the knapsacks in the front hall closet; those go in the bedrooms under the desks. Weekday coats are hung on hooks that I had put into the closet, shoes go on the floor of the closet and my husband's things go up on the top shelf. I came up with a great idea for all the little things like the wallets, baseball hats, lunch bags, and sweaters. Inside the closet I hung a shoe rack that has a few compartments, and we use these as shelves for all of our things. It's a quick way to find our belongings when we're on our way out of the house.

Tova: You make it sound so simple. It just wouldn't work in my house.

Easy-to-reach "homes" **Chani:** Tova, you should apply the principles that you used to organize your kitchen. If it only takes one to two motions to put something away, then there's a much better chance that it'll happen. After you helped me reorganize my fridge, I was so inspired I applied the same concept to other areas of my house that needed organization. I found easy-to-reach "homes" for all the stuff that comes in and goes out every day, and I saw a real improvement on the clutter barometer in my house.

Tova: You're right, Chani. I didn't realize that the incoming and outgoing stuff is a topic of its own, and needs to be addressed separately from the usual clutter around the house. I really must give it some more thought. So where do you keep everything?

Chani: I thought back to my school days when everyone *Cubby system* had a locker for all of their things, and a little light bulb went off in my head. I decided to make cubbies right near the front door for each member of my family, with doors, of course, so that the mess is hidden. So I went out and bought a short two-door closet and divided it with shelves on each side. The bottom cubby is for everyone's shoes and the other cubbies are allocated to each member of the family. For example, I keep my pocketbook, wallet and *shiur* notebook in mine, and my husband keeps his briefcase, *sefarim*, car keys and *tallis* bag in his. The older children use the cubbies for their knapsacks, lunch bags, wallets, water bottles and other outdoor stuff, like bicycle helmets and MP3 players. In the winter, they also keep their sweaters, scarves and gloves in there. I also use the kids' cubbies for things that I have to send to school with them. For example, if I have a note to send or something to return to the school, I put it in the relevant child's cubby with a note explaining what to do. This works most of the time; they'll usually notice what I put there when they're on their way out.

Sarah: It sounds more like a messy closet.

Chani: Well, it's one of my newer projects, so the details still have to be worked out. It's working well, but it would work even better if we all cleaned out our cubbies once a month to reduce the clutter buildup. Problem is — I hate that part! Also, the kids still need to be reminded to put their things in their cubbies. On the whole though, I think I'm on the right track with this idea; it's definitely keeping our stuff accessible yet out of the way.

Tova: Sounds like an amazing idea! I think I'll try it. I might even give out prizes to the kids if they cooperate nicely.

Chani: What have you been doing until now?

Tova: We have a row of labeled hooks, but only the kids' jackets and some sweaters fit on them. For a while, I had a shoe stand near the door, which did the trick until the baby noticed it and started chomping on the shoes. Keeping the shoes behind closed doors would be a better idea with a baby around, and it would also give the house a neater look. I've looked at closets made just for shoes in the furniture store, but they're pretty expensive and they're bulky, too. I really like your cubby idea; I hope it works for me.

Chani: It's really your idea, Tova! I simply took it a step further and applied the concept in a different room in the house.

Home Office

Mail, bills and advertisements

Sarah: We cannot finish this topic without discussing the home office. Let's talk about how to handle all the mail, bills, advertising clippings, medical papers, school notices, warranties and whatnot.

Chani: You've just described the door of my refrigerator.

Sarah: All those things are hanging on your fridge?

Chani: No, some things are also on a bulletin board in the kitchen, some are crammed into my husband's cubby, and the rest is piled on top of the fax machine.

Sarah: Oy, Chani! Listen, I have a great system; maybe you'll like it, too. I bought a few extra large office loose-leafs, a few packages of plastic sleeves and I created a home for every paper that lands in my house.

Loose-leaf system

Chani: Every paper?!

Sarah: Yes, every paper. Let me explain. I have two large loose-leafs for all of our medical files with section dividers for each family member. I keep vaccination records, blood reports, paperwork from doctors, prescriptions and whatever I feel is necessary to save. I keep an empty plastic sleeve in front for all up and coming appointments, pertinent documents and prescriptions. When I am looking for any recent information, I know I can find it there. Eventually I file it away in the appropriate section.

Medical file

  I have another loose-leaf with all the birth certificates, social security cards, diplomas, marriage license, *kesubah* and other official documents. I punched holes in a manila envelope to fit in the loose-leaf, and I keep everyone's passports in it.

Important documents file

  I have a fourth loose-leaf with our home and mortgage information. I keep an additional loose-leaf for bills, bank statements, gas, electric and phone bills, tax information, coupons, extra checkbooks, etc. The unpaid bills are in a sleeve in the front, and once a week we pay some

Mortgage file and finance file

bills and file it in the appropriate section.

Instructions and warranties

A very helpful file I created was an alphabetized loose-leaf for all of the warranties, direction booklets and assembly information for every appliance, electronic device and for basically everything we own. I love this file. When a swing broke off our swing set or when the rubber piece snapped on my vacuum cleaner, I was able to locate the model numbers easily in order to buy a new piece right away. When my new phone broke, I found the warranty and returned it to the store to be fixed. And, listen to this one: To my husband's delight, when we pulled out the box with the baby swing after many years in storage, I whipped out the assembly instructions. He was so impressed.

"Mommy file"

My absolute favorite file is what I call the "Mommy file." Everything that doesn't belong anywhere else, finds its way into this file — magazine clippings, advertisements, even loose notes from inspiring *shiurim*. I have a sleeve full of vacation and day trip information that I add to every year. I keep a file on how to make Pesach, I file *mishlo'ach manos* lists for Purim, some Elul ideas, my favorite birthday cards, speech therapy games to play with children… you name it, it's probably in there — in its own separate section, filed alphabetically by topic!

Before I created this file, I had all this stuff saved in the drawers of my night table. Everything was in there, but I couldn't find anything when I needed it. Now, my drawers are available for the things I need by my bedside, and all my important Mommy papers are accessible whenever I need them.

By the way, the only things I hang on my refrigerator are my calendar, my To Do list, and my running shopping list. Occasionally, there's a school notice up there too, but I try to deal with those quickly and then throw them out.

Chani: Where do you keep all these loose-leafs?

Sarah: I keep them all in a cabinet near the computer. *Location of* Storing them in your bedroom or in a kitchen cabinet *files* would work just as well. For me, the important thing is that they're accessible and near a desk or table, so that I can deal with papers as soon as they come in, even if I'm busy. I intentionally didn't create a catchall place for incoming mail and papers because I really don't like dealing with a whole pile of accumulated papers.

Tova: I do something very similar. Instead of loose-leafs, *Filing boxes* I have filing boxes for all our medical papers, bills and warranties. It does take up more space, but it's easier to flip through and file things away. I store the boxes in a filing cabinet in the kitchen. I keep an "incoming basket" on top of the cabinet, and as soon as the mail, school notice, instruction manual, or prescription comes into the house, they go straight into the basket. The inbox does get full pretty quickly, so I try to file the papers away a few times a week. But since the filing boxes are right in my kitchen, I find that it's not such a big deal to find the few minutes to take care of it.

Dena: You guys are so old-fashioned! I have most things *Computerized* filed away on my computer — like bills, mortgage and *files* medical information. All my warranties, instruction manuals and important papers are in an envelope in a drawer near the computer. Since I don't alphabetize everything, it does take me a bit longer to find things, but it doesn't bother me. A Mommy file seems like a great idea. It would sure clean out my night table!

Ripple effect   **Sarah:**   Now, that's a really good point that basically sums up our topic of organizing the home: Whichever area of the home you are organizing, there will be a ripple effect on all of the other areas of the home. Like Dena just said, if she creates a Mommy file, she'll also be clearing out room in her night table. Then she'll probably remove something that's cluttering up her closet and put it into that newly available space. Then her closet will be more organized, so she'll put the skirts that she had hung in her husband's closet back in hers. Then of course, her husband's closet will be more organized.

When I reorganized my toy shelves, I cleared up so much space that I decided to put all our sewing paraphernalia in the playroom. Moving the sewing machine from the linen closet to a playroom shelf cleared another shelf, so I moved all our home office files out of the kitchen and put them there. Wherever I start, my whole house eventually benefits.

Chani: This is all so overwhelming!

Sarah: Pick the one place that bothers you the most in your house, the place that interferes most with your day-to-day living, and start from there. Plan on doing only one project at a time; there's no rush. Allow yourself to start small and see where this ripple effect takes you. Start now and you won't believe the difference it will make in your Pesach cleaning this spring. You'll appreciate how smoothly your home will begin to run even after starting with a few little changes in home organization.

Sarah's Ten Steps to Declutter Your House

(Based on *Confessions of an Organized Housewife*
by Deniece Schofield)

1. **Pick an area** in your house where clutter most disrupts the daily functioning of your home (a closet, drawer or shelf).

2. **Decide on the purpose** of the space (for example, a cutlery drawer should contain cutlery and some utensils, but not toothpicks, bottle caps and pens, unless you have decided that they're necessary).

3. **Sort** the unnecessary items into four piles: (a) belongs somewhere else, (b) give away, (c) throw out, (d) unsure. Try to limit the number of items in the "unsure" pile.

4. **Ask yourself questions**, such as: (a) How often do I use this? (b) Is the space more precious than the item it holds? (c) Do I really need so many? (dish towels, sheets, puzzles, pens) (d) Am I ever going to fix it? (e) Will this ever fit me or come back in style?

5. **Find or create sensible "homes"** for all homeless and miscellaneous objects. Only purchase new storage solutions such as containers, drawers or baskets after giving its use much thought.

6. **Follow through** with giveaway items and with repairs which you put aside.

7. **Explain to your family** your new organizational system. Clearly label shelves and drawers so all family members know where things belong.

8. **Maintain** your organized space. Once you have decluttered a space and designated its use, it is easy to maintain.

9. **Continue decluttering** different spots around the house until you get to all of them.

10. **Prevent buildup:** Lastly, be vigilant about not allowing clutter to build up in your home in the first place. For example, get rid of newspapers and magazines as soon as your family is finished with them, and don't let clothes, coats, sweaters and shoes that aren't worn hang around.

General Organization Tips

Do your errands — Create time in your schedule. Try every two weeks or so to take care of the errands that cause clutter buildup: immersing new dishes and utensils in the *mikveh*, returning borrowed items, mending clothing, checking for *sha'atnez*, etc.

Constant maintenance — Even the most organized homes with the best systems in place don't stay that way without regular straightening up, discarding and rearranging.

Streamlining — The less stuff you have, the less messy the house gets. Keep only the things that you use and give away or junk everything else. Only store things if there is a very reasonable chance that you will use them in the future. The space is very often worth more than the items that you are saving.

Yard sales — Get together with your friends and make

money on all your extras or create a fundraiser. "One person's junk is another person's treasure."

Behind closed doors — Open shelves become messy-looking very quickly. Keep things in drawers, closets or containers for a neater look.

Keep surfaces clear — A cleared dining room table, kitchen table, coffee table and couch give the impression that the house is clean even when it is not.

Rotate toys and books — Put a third to a half in storage and rotate two to three times a year. This makes cleanup easier, keeps the toys interesting and allows for more shelf space.

Be aware — Be conscious of which messes are bothering you and schedule time to tackle them.

Keep up — Don't let daily messes build up. Start the next activity (cooking, art project, toys, etc.) only after the last one was put away. At the end of the day you will feel less overwhelmed.

Magical five minutes — A lot can be done in just five minutes, such as, a quick cleanup of a drawer or shelf in the kitchen, or a quick refolding of the contents of a drawer or shelf as you put away the clean laundry. The five minutes here and there add up, and your whole house benefits.

Delegate — Children can learn to enjoy cleaning up toys if you make it fun. A bored child might enjoy reorganizing the pantry or straightening a drawer in the kitchen.

Bath toys — Keep the toys in a net on the wall in the bathtub so that they can drip dry.

Files for kids — You can create loose-leaf files for each child so that they can save their birthday cards, pictures or stationery in an organized way.

Bag dispenser — Store plastic shopping bags in a bag dispenser near your diaper changing area and in the kitchen. A convenient place is inside the cabinet door under the sink.

Itemized storage — Keep storage boxes for every occasion in a storage room or high up in a closet.

- *Purim:* groggers, costumes, cellophane and ribbon, megillahs
- *Chanukah: Dreidel* collection, cookie cutters, menorahs, extra candles, left over Chanukah games, books and coloring books
- *Sukkos:* Decorations, *lulav* and *esrog* holders, tablecloth clips, bee trap
- *Gift box:* New baby clothing, picture frames, gifts that you never used, wrapping paper
- *Summer:* Sun hats, water bottle holders, small knapsacks for trips, bathing suits and caps, inflatable pool toys, water shoes, inflatable ball, Frisbee, kite, sun tan lotion
- *Winter:* Boots, gloves, scarves and hats

Chapter 11

Cleaning and Home Maintenance

Four Different Attitudes

What's the point?

Chani: My theory on spending time cleaning the house can basically be summed up by the magnet hanging on my fridge: "To clean the house while the children are growing is like hanging your clothes out to dry in the rain." It is totally useless! As soon as a chair is cleaned, sticky hands make it dirty again. Why chase those messes all day and wear myself out, only to be left with a mess at the end of the day anyway? Laundry and dishes are essential and must be done. Bathrooms and floors get cleaned once a week before Shabbos. But I don't have time in my day for scrubbing and shining surfaces that are going to get dirty again anyway!

Sarah: Why not? What are you so busy doing?

Taking care of basic needs

Chani: I wish I could figure that out! One thing's for sure, I don't sit around all day drinking coffee. Keeping up with the basic needs of a large family is enough to keep me busy all week long. Food shopping, cooking, changing diapers, homework help — everything takes time. Each child is a world unto himself, and besides needing my attention and guidance, needs practical care, such as transportation arrangements and appointments! Then there are my own personal needs that I must take care of.

Baruch Hashem, I think that we all have gotten so used to the idea of having large families that we forget how much effort goes into running one successfully! It's really an enormous undertaking with many details in many areas, and frankly, for me, cleaning is at the bottom of my list. I feel that it is a privilege to be raising children and I try not to let the mess get to me. It usually doesn't, and by the time it does, it's too large to tackle! I rely on Pesach cleaning to get to most areas of the house, but the truth is I usually go away for Pesach. So some cleaning projects just never happen.

I have two tips that keep my house looking passable. I keep everything behind closed doors. No open shelves, so that the mess is not staring me in the face. I also try very hard to keep my dining room, coffee and kitchen tables clear, or at least to keep the pile of stuff that accumulates during the week on one corner of the table. These are the tips I have to offer, but really I want to listen and learn something from all of you that will help me maintain my house while not conflicting with my nature or attitudes.

Keeping messes hidden

Tova: I really do think that cleaning is a personality thing. Being clean and organized doesn't come naturally to me. I used to walk around my house feeling guilty that I couldn't get to everything. I tried hiring some cleaning help, but it was so frustrating to spend all that money and have so much of my clean home become undone by my children on the very same day. I waver back and forth with the cleaning help depending on our budget. I came to the conclusion that no one notices the clean windows, clean corners under the beds or sparkling cabinet doors except me. I do the best I can to keep up with all these extras, but it's not worth my energy to get upset when I can't get to it. I try to have a home which is clean enough to be healthy, but messy enough to be happy. My home is not a museum! I want it to feel lived in. I go on cleaning binges often, but honestly it's only to make room for the next mess.

Clean enough to be healthy

Dena: Enough guilt, ladies! It sounds like both of you have been wise enough to sort through your feelings and prioritize according to your personalities. You both are doing great jobs running your large, thriving families, and

No guilt approach

there's no reason to feel guilty over a mess. That's my attitude when it comes to cleaning — if it bothers me, I make the time to clean it myself or get someone else to do it. If it's unrealistic to get the cleaning done, then I leave it, and I'm okay with it. I let the important stuff aggravate me, like children or work issues — not dust balls.

Tova: What a liberating concept! You're right. I have enough places to put my guilty feelings. But Dena, you're busier than all of us. When do you find the time to get to all the extras?

Necessary cleaning help

Dena: Cleaning help is a must for me. You're right, Tova, the house gets messy again quickly, but having regular cleaning help does make a difference. The kids can't ruin every corner of the house in one day, and the once-a-week help keeps my house in better shape.

Cleaning the extras

As for extras, I only clean what bothers me when it bothers me. If I'm sitting on the couch and I see a layer of dust building up on my ceiling fan, I'll write it down on my list and at some point that week, I'll find a few minutes to get to it. I won't stare at it for months and months saying, "What can I do, I have no time to get rid of the dirt!"

Breaking down big jobs

My biggest tip is that I break every big job down into stages. If I want to wash the curtains, one night I'll take out the ladder, the next night I'll take down the curtains and the next day I'll throw them into the washing machine. I don't have large blocks of time to dedicate to cleaning. As a working mother, I use this tip for everything — cooking, organizing, and just about any home project.

Making time for home improvement

I save vacations for home improvement projects that require more time to do. It may be painting a room, redoing the storage closet, re-organizing the playroom...

Over time, everything in the house basically gets taken care of. I enjoy living in a well-kept home and I find that my family functions better when everything is clean and in its place. It gives the message that the people who live in this house are important and are cared for.

Chani: I am inspired, but the thought of tackling all these projects is truly overwhelming. I don't really believe it's possible, and besides, I don't really have the time!

Dena: Trust me — you can make time for anything that you feel is important enough to make time for. Take it from a working mother of a large family! The winter months have less action in them, since there are no *Yamim Tovim* or extended vacations when the children are home. This is the perfect time to dedicate at least a month or two to a major and thorough cleaning of different areas of the house. Pick the spot that bothers you the most or that frightens you the least, and start there. Once it's clean, it's really not so hard to maintain. Once a week, I have my cleaning help go through one room in the house more thoroughly so that the hidden dirt and the mess buildup is only a few weeks worth and not a few months.

Winter is a great time

Sarah, you're being too quiet! Your house is always spotless. How do you manage to keep it so clean?

Sarah: I wouldn't say it's spotless, but I do work at keeping it clean and organized. I can't even relate to what Chani and Tova have been saying. I personally can't function when my house is dirty and can't think straight when it is cluttered. I walk around all day picking things up off the floor and putting them away. As soon as I see an item is no longer in use, it gets thrown in the garbage. As I cook, I straighten up some kitchen drawers and organize the pantry.

A clean house is a prerequisite

Tova: There you go, again. We're talking about cleaning. Not decluttering and organizing.

Organization and cleanliness go together

Sarah: It's one and the same. You can't separate it. If there is no clutter, the house stays clean. Dusting, sweeping and wiping all take seconds if there are no extra things around and everything is organized and in its place. My friends are convinced that I must scrub all day to keep my house clean, but it's not true at all. I actually rarely have to scrub anything. I wipe up spills as soon as they happen and wash the dishes before the food hardens on them. I put away my ingredients and my pots after I cook, so it takes just a second to wipe the counter down. I train my children to put the laundry in the basket as soon as they shower, so there is no clutter of clothing all over the house. If they don't do it, I do it. The shoes also go in their designated place as soon as they are taken off. Without all the clutter around the house, it's seems effortless to sweep up a few crumbs or wipe up a dirty floor with a rag. I often don't use any cleaning solutions, just water.

Tova: So you are in constant motion, always decluttering and picking up. Doesn't that get annoying? And what happens when you're not around?

Regular cleanup

Sarah: It's true that it's constant, but it's not overwhelming because everything in my house has a place. I don't feel that I'm cleaning all day; it just comes naturally to me. I prefer to be constantly straightening up little messes than to be faced with a big one at the end of the day. It has to be cleaned up at some point. When I've been out, you can tell by looking at my house, but it never looks like it was hit by a hurricane. Since I am always on top of the situation, the buildup is minimal. My husband and children are not used to seeing such large messes, so when I have a baby or go away for a longer period of time, even they wake up and start straightening up.

There was a time when I had to stay in the hospital with one of my children for an extended period. As I said, I can't function when my house is dirty and cluttered and it was very difficult for me to manage. I got extra cleaning help and gave out more jobs to my children, but truth be told, I had to let go of my standards a little. It was very hard for me to let go, because keeping clean has become so much a part of me. I could have used some tips then for how to run a household, even with a mess.

Managing in a crisis

I am also very particular about rules. When the family abides by my rules, a lot of cleaning work is avoided. I see myself as a "friendly policeman." Rule #1 is: Food stays only in the kitchen! It takes some effort to keep to this rule, but it is well worth it. I never have to clean out toys, sheets, floors, drawers from crumbs and sticky messes. I also avoid ant problems this way. I even put a gate on my kitchen so that I won't have to keep on reminding my little ones to eat there. In the kitchen, the kids don't have to sit at the table; I allow them to walk around with a snack. As long as the crumbs stay in the kitchen, I don't mind sweeping often. Occasionally, I allow the older children to eat an apple or non-crumby food out of the kitchen as long as they are careful about throwing out their garbage afterwards.

Abiding by rules

Another rule that I'm particular about is that everyone must do their after-dinner chore. One child clears the table, one washes the dishes and one folds laundry. I even started training my 5-year old to sweep the floor with a kiddy broom and dust pan. Every little bit helps me and also raises their consciousness to keeping a clean house.

I try to keep to the "One toy at a time" rule. It works most of the time, but sometimes when there is an intense game of House or Store, they seem to need every item in the house for their game! When the boys build with blocks, they need the Clics, cars and Little People to complete their city. I suggest that these creative play hours take place in a bedroom or playroom, but I don't forbid them from playing in the living room. When I see that the game is really over, I make sure that they all clean up.

Tova: You probably don't let your children play with Play-doh, bake cookies, paint or things like that.

Allowing supervised messes

Sarah: To be honest, it doesn't thrill me, but I try hard not to stifle them because of my own need to be clean. I put a disposable tablecloth on the table, make sure that they remain in the kitchen or playroom and stay close by so things don't get out of hand. I would never take a nap or go out while my kids are painting, unless I have a really responsible child watching over them.

Dena: Do you have cleaning help?

Sarah: I do hire help before Pesach, but otherwise, I do everything myself, the way I like it to be done.

Dena: Well then, you must teach us all your secrets to keeping a clean house.

Tips for Different Areas of the House

Sarah: I'll be happy to teach you all the tricks I know in heavy and light housekeeping and home maintenance. I'm assuming you all know how to do the basics, so I'll just give you some pointers.

Chani: Don't assume anything!

Sarah: I do a thorough cleaning of my house once a week giving more attention to a different area each time (see page 157). I buy one good quality big jerry can of an all-purpose cleaner, such as Fantastic or Ajax, and I use that for everything. I even keep some diluted with water, in a spritz bottle. I generally don't waste money on different sprays and specific cleaners for different areas of the house, unless I really see that it makes a difference. I buy a good quality dish soap which I use often to clean counters, floors and to get greasy stains out of the laundry. I find myself using wet wipes to clean surfaces nicely and quickly. I think I may use them more on the house than on the baby!

One all-purpose cleaner

The latest rag on the market is one made out of microfiber. I use them on all parts of my house since they clean very thoroughly and leave a nice finish. I keep a dairy one and meat one to wipe down counters and tables and I hang them over the sink to dry. I have another one handy to wipe down chairs and walls. I rinse them out in the sink with dish soap or bleach. Once a week I wash them all in the washing machine.

Microfiber rags

Let's start with the kitchen. I try to wash my dishes as soon as the meal is over. It takes just a few minutes when all the food particles are still wet. If I can't get to them soon enough, I plug up the sink and fill it with soapy water. By the time I get to them the dishes are practically clean. A good dishwashing liquid goes a long way. I find it's more economical to buy an expensive brand than a diluted cheaper one.

Kitchen: Dealing with dishes

Tova: I hate washing dishes. I let them pile up till the evening and then have a dishwashing session with one of my girls.

Chani: As long as you get to it, that's what counts.

Lining counters   **Sarah:**   When I'm cooking something that's very messy or when I'm about to cook a lot at once, I line my kitchen counter with a disposable table cloth. I wet the counter a little bit so that the table cloth will stick to it. When I am all finished, I just roll up the tablecloth and the counters are clean.

Maintaining range and oven   The hardest parts of the kitchen to clean are the range and the oven. I usually leave the lining from Pesach on the range and change it when I can no longer wipe it down easily. Sometimes I use oven liners. The best thing to do is just to wipe the range and oven with a damp, microfiber cloth after every use before the spills get cooked in. If they don't come off easily, I let it soak in a cleaning solution for 5-10 minutes and then wipe it away. I save oven cleaner for *erev* Pesach, since it is too strong for regular use. It's worth the few minutes it takes when I finish cooking to clean up after myself to avoid intense cleaning later on.

Wiping fridge regularly   The same goes for the fridge. I'm constantly wiping parts of it down and almost never cleaning it. Leftovers either get eaten the next day or put into the freezer to be used at a different time. Old fruits, vegetables and residue are thrown out before the fruit and vegetable drawer gets restocked. By having a clutter-free fridge, I can identify spills immediately and clean them up before they cake up. In the event that the mess in the fridge does get out of hand, soaking the shelves in a bathtub full of cleaning liquid and water takes care of the problem easily.

Tops of cabinets   It's unhealthy to breathe in years of dust sitting on the top of the kitchen cabinets. Every year during Pesach cleaning, I buy a roll of plastic tablecloth and tape it down to the top of my kitchen cabinets. The following year, I roll it up and throw it out with all the dust. I never clean there any more.

Tova: What I can't see doesn't bother me.

Dena: I had a built-in soffit between the tops of my kitchen cabinets and the ceiling so there's no place for dust to accumulate.

Let's move on to the bathroom. Do you have any good ideas to get the bad odor out of the bathroom? Even after my cleaning lady leaves, the main bathroom still has that bad smell.

Sarah: I don't have so many little boys around, which makes a big difference. But what works well is to splash a nice-smelling cleaning solution all over the outside of the toilet, the walls near the toilet, and anything within range of the toilet. Let the cleaner sink into the walls and exchange smells with the bad one. After about twenty minutes to a half an hour, wipe it up and the bathroom will smell fresh.

Bathrooms: Keeping them fresh

Tova: I like to spritz cleaner all around and let it sit for a few minutes. I then take the shower head and give the entire bathroom a complete shower, being careful not to get the cabinets very wet. The water gets into all the cracks and crevices behind the toilet and under the cabinets and all the dirt and smells get washed away. I then push all the water down the hall and out the yard door. Of course, this won't work for everyone; it depends on the layout of your house or apartment. But I like doing it this way because the hall gets a good washing at the same time. When I have a little less time, I sweep the water into an extra large dustpan, dump it into a bucket, and then flush it.

Dena: Both your ideas sound good. What do you do about wet towel buildup?

Wet towels **Sarah:** My younger children alternate taking baths every other day, so I never have all the towels wet at once. I hang their towels, open, over the shower door or over the towel bars with the window open. When they dry, I hang them back on the hook. I wash them once a week.

Chani: My younger children share towels. So, it's only a few bath towels that have to dry. The kids are clean anyway after a bath! It also cuts down on the laundry.

Tova: I'm into bathrobes after their bath instead of towels. It covers more and keeps them warmer after a bath. Each child has his own bathrobe and hangs it to dry over a chair in his room after his bath. Then it's supposed to go back on the hook. I wash them when they don't smell fresh anymore.

Mold and **Sarah:** To prevent mold and mildew buildup, I hang the
mildew shower and floor mats on separate hooks after every use, to air out. I don't let them sit on the wet floor. I always keep the window open to allow the moisture to evaporate more quickly. After all the children finish bathing, I try to give a quick wipe to the bathtub doors and walls to get rid of the excess water. I painted my bathroom ceilings and corners with a special quality, anti-mold paint, made specifically for bathrooms and places prone to mold and mildew buildup. It works pretty well. I use a bleach pen to get rid of the mold on the grout between the tiles. There were a few spots where the mold just wouldn't come out and I had to scratch it out and re-grout it or re-silicone it around the bathtub.

Tova: I must share with you how my plumber taught me how to unclog sinks. You won't believe how simple it is!

Clogged sinks

I deal with it as soon as I notice the water drainage is slower than usual, before it gets completely stuffed up. I take a disposable skewer stick and poke around down the drain, pushing down whatever is stuck there. It is usually soft things like soap and hair. In the kitchen, it is usually just food particles. As the gunk moves down, the pipe's opening expands so that the pieces can move down more easily. Then I run a strong stream of hot or boiling water to wash it away. Periodically, I sprinkle baking soda down the drains, followed by some vinegar. The bubbling chemical reaction breaks up all the dirt stuck to the pipes and then a strong boiling stream of water from the kettle washes it away.

Dena: My plumber told me not to strain my noodles or to pour out oil from the frying pan down the sink. It sticks to the sides of the pipes and forms a paste causing other particles to stick to it and clog the narrow pipe.

Chani: Really! So where do you strain your noodles?

Dena: I haven't come up with such a good solution. I strain it into a huge bowl and dump it outside. I pour the oil from the frying pan into a baggie and throw it into the garbage.

Sarah: What great ideas! The baking soda/vinegar idea probably also gets rid of all those bad smells lurking in the pipes.

Okay, no sidetracking. Let's finish up with the bathrooms.

Faucets   I find that there is always calcium buildup around the faucets. I use a special hard water cleaning spray for this, since no other cleaning liquid does the job. A few spritzes and a quick scrub, and my faucets look like new.

Constant maintenance   My final tip for the bathroom is just to check it out often. I've gotten into the habit of wiping down the counters, the inside of the sink, the toilet seat and the underside of the toilet seat with a wet wipe every time I walk in there. Just be sure not to throw the wipes in the toilet, as that causes major pipe problems. I also use the shower head to give the inside of the toilet a rinse, to wash the dirty residue before it hardens. I installed a toilet douche—which is like a tiny shower head near the toilet—specifically for this purpose.

Chani: I keep nice-smelling potpourri on the counter to keep the bathroom smelling sweet and fresh. I enjoy experimenting with all the different products and new smells on the market.

Let's move on to our next topic—floors. How do you keep your floor so clean, Sarah?

Floors: Different cleaning methods   **Sarah:** There are so many different styles of washing the floor and so many different types of mops on the market. I use what is most comfortable for me and easiest to clean. Some people like to use lots of water and push it all out the door. This does do a thorough cleaning, but, aside from making a big mess and possibly ruining the furniture, it wastes a lot of water. Here's what I do for a thorough floor cleaning. First I sweep and then I wash each section of the floor twice. The first washing is a superficial one to loosen up all the dirt. I leave a thin film of soapy water on the floor, but no big puddles. I then do a more thorough washing of the same section using a bit more muscle, washing away all the dirt. I wash out my cloth or mop head after each major section. I use a separate microfiber cloth to dry the floor for a polished finish.

Every once in a while, after the first superficial wash, I take a hard bristle scrub brush and get down on my hands and knees to scrub in between the tiles and in the corners where the walls meet the floor. Then I wash all the dirt away with the second washing. This might scratch up some floors, so test it out in a hidden area.

Chani: So that's what those things are for! I've seen that hard bristle broom-sized brush attached to a stick and I couldn't figure out why they would make a broom with such hard bristles. Sarah, it would probably be easier to use that than getting down on your hands and knees.

Sarah: You're right. You must tell me where you've seen that.

Dena: I vacuum up all the dust in the corners of the floor with a tube extension of the vacuum cleaner. I also use this attachment to do a quick cleaning of the bottom of the closets.

Sarah: Speaking of floors, does anyone have any tips on how to get rid of ants? I have a crawling baby and I don't want to use an exterminator.

Keeping ants away

Chani: I also don't like to spray my house with unnecessary poison. I'm at constant battle with the ants, but I'm winning. I simply keep sealing up their holes. I make a paste with plaster powder from the hardware store and water and seal it up with spackling compound. Once the ants see that they can't get food from that location, they leave. The key is to keep sealing up the holes till they get the message. For extra protection, I put some rosemary or sprinkle semolina on the floor near their hole. Supposedly, it keeps them away.

Dena: There are some great ant traps on the market that really work. If you can put them in an area that little children can't get to, it will take care of your ant problem without extermination or daily sealing up of holes.

Of course, regular sweeping also helps, since crumbs attract ants. As long as you keep sweeping, the ants won't be able to find food and they'll go elsewhere.

Walls and doors

Tova: You know, even when my house is spotless after a thorough *erev* Shabbos cleaning, it still doesn't sparkle because my walls are dirty. I guess it's really time to paint.

Dena: If you do decide to paint, then spend the extra money and get a good washable paint. You'll be able to clean smudges and dirt with just a wipe, especially if you use a "wonder sponge." For permanent marker stains or other stains that don't come off with a wet sponge, you can keep a can of extra paint handy; it's really easy to do small touch-ups.

Regular whitewashing

Sarah: I don't use the washable paint. Instead, every half a year or so, we whitewash the walls just up to the height of my oldest son's head. That's where there's a concentration of oily handprints and footprints and Matchbox car wheel marks!

Tova: Why haven't you ever painted professionally? That's so unlike you!

Sarah: You know, clean white walls give the house a fresh look. I want to be able to paint often, and if I would have it painted professionally, I would get stressed when a child dirties the walls. Whitewash is the cheapest and easiest way to go. It dries in an hour or two and blends in with the previous paint job so that I don't have to paint the entire wall. Also, if the whitewash gets on the floor, it comes off easily — no turpentine necessary.

I find that my walls get nicked from all sorts of things, from tantrums to arts and crafts projects to rearranging the pictures on the walls. I fix these up with some plaster and whitewash; it's really simple. If you really like color, dye can be added to the whitewash, but then you have to paint up to the ceiling and it becomes a job. I have been considering adding some color in some of the less-used rooms.

Even though I repaint often, I also wipe down the walls with the wonder sponge whenever I see a smudge, so that the dirt doesn't build up.

I use corner guards for all the wall corners in the house. These come in all colors, are easy to install and give the room a finished look.

Tova: How do you get rid of sticky remnants of tape? We hang our kids' pictures up on the windows and some of the doors and I can't get those marks off.

Removing sticky tape

Sarah: Goo Gone, WD40, acetone, and paint thinner all get rid of those sticky spots. These do the trick for remnants of tape in your cabinets and fridge after Pesach.

Chani: Nobody has mentioned getting rid of cobwebs. Once in awhile, as an activity, my children walk around with a broom, knocking out cobwebs from the corners of all the ceilings.

Any good advice for keeping the bedrooms clean? For me, the children's rooms are the hardest to keep clean.

Bedrooms **Sarah:** Bedrooms take more self-discipline to clean. Since the kitchen is used all day long, by necessity it has to be cleaned up. Bedrooms, on the other hand, are basically used for sleeping, and as long as there's room to sleep, it's easy to ignore the mess. But my nature doesn't allow me to leave it a mess for long.

Chani: You wouldn't appreciate the collection of stuff my kids sleep with on their beds!

Sarah: What really bugs me is that when there's a buildup of clutter in the bedroom, it's impossible to dust and vacuum. It's really important to have some kind of system of organization in the bedroom especially if there are a few children sharing a room. With all the clean and dirty clothes, slippers and shoes, toys and books, and *chatchkes*, the room can get out of control pretty quickly.

Morning cleanup In my house, my children have to straighten up their room before they go to school in the morning. If they do, they get a special treat for school. Of course, there's always something left for me to finish up, but at least it's manageable. The most important principle in the kids' bedrooms is that each child must have easy access to his own personal space, so that it's not hard for them to put their things away. It's also helpful if the hamper is in a convenient spot so that it's easy for the kids to throw their dirty laundry in there, and they're not tempted to leave it around. Lastly, I try not to store things under the beds. If I must, I make sure to keep it in one large box or container for easy moving and cleaning.

Once there's no clutter, dusting, sweeping and vacuuming only takes a few minutes — really! And once a week is sufficient.

Chani: I think it would work out better for me if my kids cleaned up in the evening.

Sarah: It doesn't really matter, as long as it's in their schedule and it's not all left for you to do.

Changing linens

I change all the sheets once a week. I'm always amazed at how much sand and dirt gets into the kids' beds in one week! Changing the sheets often also cuts down on the amounts of treasures my children can store under their pillows. I find that fresh smelling sheets help them sleep better. I wash and dry them and then put them right back on the bed to avoid folding them.

Dena: Every other week is enough for me! I don't have the extra time or energy to huff and puff over blanket covers and fluffing up pillows every week.

Tova: What's the point of washing them on a schedule? With young children, the sheets get washed often enough because they get soiled in some way. The older kids put their sheets in the laundry when they feel like it, and I can trust them to do it because they're already sensitive to cleanliness. I don't think it's necessary to make sheet changing an official part of my schedule. I do it on an as-needed basis.

Chani: Haven't we covered everything? What's left?

Sarah: Windows! I don't bother with them on a regular basis, unless someone really smudges them up. Once or

Windows and screens

twice a year, I do a thorough cleaning of the screens and windows.

There are two different methods that I use. On a sunny day, I remove the removable part of the window and screen and shower them down in the bathtub. Before putting them back, I use a toothbrush to get into the small cracks of the frame. I wash the dirt out with water and then wipe it down. Since this makes a big mess, I sometimes just loosen the dirt with a dry toothbrush and then just vacuum the dirt out with the vacuum hose.

When I don't feel like removing the windows, I wipe the screen down with a wet cloth removing all the dirt. I bought this neat little magnetic gadget that has two window wipers that stick to each other on two sides of the window. As I clean the inside of the window, the wiper does the same on the outside of the window. It does a pretty thorough job, but not as good as using the bathtub. It is definitely more fun to use.

Chani: All of this information is very useful, but it's making me nervous! Can we move on to a different topic?

Tova: You know, Chani, there are different stages of life when it's easier or harder to focus on being clean and organized. When my energy level is low due to a pregnancy or after having a baby, I drop all my standards and just focus on giving my children their much-needed attention. During these times, as long as there's food to eat and clean clothing to wear, I feel very accomplished.

Sarah, your tips are really useful. I really hope to improve on what I can when it's the right time for me and my family.

What to Clean

Air conditioner — Vacuum and wash vents and filters of central air conditioner. This gives the air conditioner a longer life span.

Baby carriage — Wash removable pad in machine, clean out basket from crumbs. Alternatively, the whole carriage can be showered down in the bathtub.

Bentchers — Wipe down covers.

Bookcases — Dust with wet rag. Don't forget higher shelves.

Booster seat — Take apart; clean out crumbs and wipe down.

Ceiling fans — Wipe down fins with wet rag or wet wipes.

Chairs — Wipe down with damp cloth; polish.

Closets — Vacuum or wipe clean the bottoms.

Couches — Vacuum/wipe down with damp cloth.

Curtains — Machine wash or dry clean.

Dining room table — Wipe down.

Door handles — Wipe down with soapy rag.

Doors — Wipe down with a sponge (try using a wonder sponge) and soapy water.

Fans — Remove outer case and rinse in tub, wipe down fins (spray with WD40 on the motor to extend life of fan).

Fridge, freezer and oven, exterior — Wipe down with microfiber cloth and dish soap.

Front door and door frame — Wipe down with wonder sponge.

Garbages — Wash every so often with bleach. Keeping

numerous bags inside protects garbage can from getting dirty.

Hampers — Clean from crumbs and dirt.

High-chair — Remove tray; clean crumbs from tray and chair; vacuum/wipe down.

Kitchen cabinets and closets, exterior — Soap and wonder sponge. Pay close attention to tops of doors and around the handles.

Kitchen drawers — Empty, and vacuum out or wipe up crumbs.

Light fixtures — Remove glass and wash out from little bugs and dust.

Light switches and outlets — Wipe down.

Microwave — Wipe down inside and outside.

Pictures — Dust with damp rag.

Plants — Rinse fake and real plants from dust in the shower or sink.

Porch — Utilize water after a rain and wipe down porch. This takes seconds.

Shelves/drawers — Wipe down as you put away laundry.

Silver — Polish. Clean out wax/oil from candlesticks with hot water and dish soap.

Toilet and toilet paper holder tops — Wipe down.

Toys, large, such as cars and kitchen set — Wipe down from dust.

Washing machine — Wipe down outside surfaces and underside of lid with wet towel.

Yard — Pick up garbage that blows in. Sweep and trim, as applicable.

Tova's Ten Step System for Delegating Housework to Children

1. **Invitations** — Place a cute invitation on each potential helper's bed inviting them to an important family meeting. Make sure to write, "Special refreshments will be served."

2. **Overdose on the positive** — Begin your meeting with lots of specific detailed compliments to each child and describe how much each one gives you so much *nachas*. Make sure to give larger than usual servings of ice cream and sprinkles or whatever special refreshments you're serving.

3. **Explain the purpose of the meeting** — Compare your household to a large and growing workplace. Describe how each employee has a different job, since it's impossible for one person to do everything that is needed for the business to run smoothly. Since your family is *baruch Hashem* growing, and there is so much that needs to be done — such as meals, laundry, dishes, and cleaning — everyone's involvement is needed. Explain how when there are fewer chores for you to do, you have more time to spend with each of them (and make sure that you do!).

4. **Make the announcement** — Announce that the purpose of the meeting is to give out mandatory daily jobs to each child to be done at a specified time. Ask children if they prefer a rotating system where they are assigned a different job every day (using a wheel or chart), or a monthly system where they have the same job every day, to be reevaluated at the end of the

month (or week). Explain that both systems have benefits — changing every day can be fun, while establishing a method in one area and perfecting it gets the job done quicker.

5. **Present job options** — Tell them which chores you have in mind and ask each child to give you his four top choices in order of preference. Also ask which job they absolutely don't want to do (only one). Take notes. Tell them that you will do your best to give them the job(s) of their choice.

6. **Be open to children's suggestions** — A child might suggest a chore that he enjoys that didn't occur to you, like polishing the silver or ironing. Anything the children can do to improve the functioning and cleanliness of the home is helpful. If they are excited about doing a particular job, it might be worth considering it and training them.

7. **Surprises** — Tell them you will surprise them with "Mommy's helper's parties" like this one every so often with treats or prizes for all the helpers. Have them each write up a list of inexpensive presents that they would appreciate getting as a reward, and choose from these. Alternatively, by doing their chores, they can accumulate points that add up to a big family prize after a few months, such as a trip or a new family toy or game. You could also offer to do a combination of both ideas.

8. **The earlier the better** — Remember, your goal is twofold: to delegate your housework as well as to teach the children responsibility. It's worthwhile to start them young even if they don't do a perfect job. Even a five-

year-old can sweep with a children's broom and learn to do a pretty thorough job. Soon they'll be your greatest helpers.

9. **Constant compliments** — Remind them regularly how many different *mitzvos* they are doing with their one act of help: *chessed, kibbud av va'eim*, making others happy and comfortable, preparing for Shabbos, etc.

10. **Work with numbers** — If you feel the chore system is too complicated, an alternative way to delegate cleanup is to set a timer before dinner (or other designated time) and have the children clean up as many items as they can. Or simply tell children to find twenty to thirty things to clean up in the room of your choice.

Some Examples of Age Appropriate Jobs

Ages 5–7: Pick up toys, wipe down chairs/tables, sweep with kid-sized broom, entertain/feed younger children, make beds, wipe down outside of cabinets, set table.

Ages 8–10: All of the above plus take out the garbage, wash dishes, peel vegetables, fold laundry and put it away, prepare younger siblings for bath.

Ages 11 and up: All of the above plus ironing, doing a load of laundry, cleaning up counters, making family's sandwiches, giving younger children baths, making dinner, vacuuming, washing kitchen floor, cleaning mirrors.

Chapter 12

Pesach

Note: There are various opinions concerning how to clean for Pesach and how to render *chametz* inedible. Please ask your own Rav before relying on the suggestions below.

Cleaning Schedules and Tips

Chani: No matter how I try to simplify Pesach and no matter how laid-back I aim to be, I have finally realized that there is no avoiding it — making Pesach is an ordeal! It takes a tremendous amount of organization and planning skills, which are not my forte. I am looking for some great ideas to help take the pressure off of preparations without ruining the atmosphere in my home. It seems to me that most women are either neurotic, starting their cleaning too early, or irresponsible, finishing (or not finishing) too late. Honestly, I do my best to go away for Pesach or get invited out because I don't feel capable of creating the right balance.

Spring cleaning till Purim only

Sarah: I can relate. It has taken me many years to come up with a system that works for me. Every Pesach I improve in a new area. I'm happy to share with you my scheduling ideas that I've formulated over the years and the helpful tips I've accumulated along the way.

For my own clarity, I have divided the preparations into three different pockets of time. The first is the end of winter, until Purim. This is the time for spring cleaning areas in the house which need major organizing (like junk drawers, closets, important paper files or cookbook shelf).

I don't want spring cleaning to slow me down during my actual Pesach cleaning. Also, if I intend to buy any new furniture or appliances before Pesach, this is the time to do the research. The result of taking care of these things in February and March is that both my home and mind get cleared so that I will be ready to clean for Pesach when the time comes.

The day after Purim is when Stage Two begins. This is when I start cleaning specifically for Pesach. My goal from Purim until Rosh Chodesh Nisan is to accomplish as much actual Pesach preparations as I can without interfering with my family's regular routine; there will be plenty of that as we get closer to Pesach. *Not disrupting family routines*

My first Pesach job is always to clean the toys we'll be using on Pesach. Then I put them out of reach where they'll stay clean and *chametz*-free. When the toys come out on Yom Tov after a month of hiding, the kids really enjoy playing with them. It's an easy first accomplishment towards Pesach.

During these two weeks, I shop for all the Yom Tov clothing, cook for the week before Pesach and for Shabbos HaGadol, clean my own closet, and mend and iron Yom Tov clothing. As it gets closer to Rosh Chodesh Nisan, I get more involved in the actual *chametz* cleaning in the more active parts of the house, like the children's closets, the deep freezer, and the upper kitchen cabinets (see page 166). I also gradually become more careful about serving *chametz*. During these two weeks, I do not create daily deadlines. I don't want to disrupt my routine too much yet. Every few days, I check my list to make sure I have made many Pesach accomplishments.

Pesach Job Suggestions between Purim and Rosh Chodesh Nisan

- Separate *chametz* from non-*chametz* items in the pantry. Notice what needs to be finished.
- Clean selected toys and put away.
- Clean master bedroom closets.
- Have children do their drawers and desks.
- Clean night tables.
- Cook meals for the two Shabbosos and for the week before Pesach.
- Defrost and clean deep freezer.
- Clean selected parts of children's closets.
- Clean junk drawer.
- Clean attic/basement (if necessary).
- Clean laundry room.
- Buy Pesach items that you need — pots, peelers, etc.
- Buy Yom Tov clothing — including socks, tights, etc.
- Buy *afikoman* presents and/or Pesach toys.
- Write all Pesach lists — menu/shopping/*mechiras chametz*/recipes.
- Mend and iron Pesach clothing.
- Clean upper kitchen cabinets.
- Polish candlesticks (closer to Rosh Chodesh).
- Clean flour sifter.
- Clean hand mixer.

From Rosh Chodesh Nisan until Seder night is "full speed ahead" with Pesach cleaning! I plan these days wisely. I sit down with a calendar and work backwards. I aim to have two full days of cooking before the day of *bi'ur chametz*. If *leil haSeder* is on a Wednesday night, that means I'd like to start cooking by Monday morning. In other words, I have to be ready to turn over (*kasher* and line the cabinets and counters) by Sunday morning. If you look at the calendar, that leaves me just nine days to finish the entire house. This is possible if these days are completely dedicated to Pesach preparations. Some of the smaller jobs can even be done on *motza'ei* Shabbos. I divide all the Pesach preparations that are left among these nine days. I like to go room by room, finishing a room in its entirety and then crossing it off the list. It's really not so difficult because so many tasks have already been done beforehand. For example, on the first day of Nisan, I'll finish the master bedroom; the closets and night tables have, hopefully, already been done. What's left are the sheets, beds, floor, a bit of laundry, windows, lock up what I am not cleaning — FINISHED!

On the second of Nisan, I do the same in one or two bedrooms. The children's desks and bookshelves should have been done already in Adar, so I just give them a quick check and I'm finished. I don't usually do all of this by myself. I hire cleaning help or get some family members to help so it goes quickly.

I also keep a list of smaller, important jobs for when I have half an hour to an hour available — like the toaster, microwave, main kitchen cabinet, phone shelf, or toy kitchen set. When someone in the house has a small amount of time, they check the list and pick a job that they can finish.

During this stage of the cleaning, I do push myself to keep daily deadlines. We keep plugging ahead till we finish the whole house. Cooking for the family is not on the schedule anymore. The Shabbos HaGadol *seudah* and a few other nutritious meals are already in my freezer from Adar. The rest of my meals consist of pasta, pizza, yogurts, sandwiches, processed, instant and canned foods. I cut up vegetable sticks if I get a chance. We'll go out to eat once or twice when we are actually turning over. Although I don't usually support such an unbalanced diet, there is a time and a place for everything.

My most helpful hint for cleaning on Pesach is that I don't let my children walk around the house with crumbly or sticky food during the year. I have trained my children that all food stays in the kitchen. They can walk around with food in the kitchen, but only in the kitchen. I discipline with a smile. If a child leaves the kitchen with food, I gently take it away from him and hand it back when he returns to the kitchen. Since I am very consistent, they catch on quickly. Once I initiated this rule, I have rarely found *chametz* in the rest of the house during my Pesach cleaning.

Chani: I think that's why Pesach cleaning is so stressful for me. I find crumbs everywhere! Although I don't enjoy being a policeman, I can understand why this one rule might be worth the energy. My kids walk around with *pekalech* all afternoon!

Sarah: Here is one more great tip. I keep a Pesach folder with all my lists from year to year. I don't pack it away with the Pesach stuff. I keep it handy so I'll have it while I'm preparing. I practically don't have to think anymore. I have my big shopping list, recipes and menus, my *mechiras chametz* list of which cabinets and rooms I'm locking up, a list of *chametz*-free meals and snacks that work for my family, my basic cleaning schedule and cleaning lists, meat and vegetable order and amounts of matzah, matzah meal and wine. These already-prepared lists eliminate much unnecessary anxiety for me. I update all of my lists on *motza'ei* Pesach according to the number of guests and family members at our table that year. As I'm sure I mentioned before, I keep similar folders for all Yamim Tovim and occasions.

Dena: These are great tips and ideas, but I couldn't possibly keep to such an intense cleaning schedule. I work up until a few days before Pesach! I also keep a very defined pre-Pesach schedule, but I do things a bit differently.

I actually tackle the kitchen first. I turn my kitchen *Tackling the* over completely, early on, by Rosh Chodesh Nisan. The *kitchen first* kitchen is the hardest and most important place to clean, so I like to do it when I have the most energy and time. I can already cook for my family and we can eat like normal people while everyone else is starving. I set up a *chametz* section with our toaster and an electric burner on the patio or in the playroom. We eat all our noodles, sandwiches and cereal there, and I'm extremely careful about the crumbs. After Rosh Chodesh Nisan, I take care of the rest of the house, comforted by the idea that the most important part of the house is done already. Whatever I don't end up getting to, I sell with the *chametz*.

I simplify cleaning as much as I can. When I go through *Simplifying* everyone's closets, I clean the exact amount of clothing my *cleaning* family will need for those eight days and I put everything else away. I don't clean toys; rather, I have a separate Pesach stash of toys and games which I add to every year. Most importantly, wherever there may possibly be *chametz* in the house, I spritz with cleaning spray so it becomes inedible and *halachically* permitted to keep on Pesach. I simply don't have time to scrub if it's not necessary.

Doing big jobs early   I make Pesach purchases very early on. I clean a high shelf in a closet and store the new Pesach items up there. Pesach is always on my mind and I shop whenever I get a chance, even on the way home from work or on Sundays. Actually, the first area I clean for Pesach is the trunk of my car where I also store things until the kitchen is ready.

My sister works full time and has an even busier schedule than mine. She invested in a Pesach kitchen in her basement. It's a wise investment if you have the space and the money. I have another sister who is a big believer in doing the bigger jobs early on such as the fridge, freezer and then lining the shelves for the next month or so. One year, she even had her cleaning help do her dining room table early on. She then wrapped it well, and all she had to do right before Pesach was unwrap it, do a quick check and wipe.

Another thing we both do is lock up parts of the house completely and sell the *chametz* in them, like the attic, basement, or even the playroom. I don't check these places at all.

I am also a big list maker. For me, just being aware of what needs to be done for Pesach keeps me calm and I tackle my list whenever I find the time. After my lists have been made, all that's left is to try my utmost, *daven* and hope for the best.

Tova: You seem to have really figured out what works for you. I can't afford a Pesach kitchen and I could never turn my kitchen over so early before Pesach. That wouldn't work for my kids or for my nerves!

I have a different plan to get the kitchen ready quickly. I clean and check my kitchen, but I don't go crazy. I lock up all my cabinets except for a few pantry shelves, which I line. Then I wheel out my Pesach cabinet from storage! I had it built by a carpenter. The bottom contains drawers for cutlery, kitchen gadgets, towels, recipe books, and *bentchers*, and the top has shelves for pots, dishes, containers, paper goods and everything else. I unlock it, and presto, I am set up to start cooking with no preparation.

My neighbor loved the idea and she did the same thing with a plastic, do-it-yourself two-door cabinet and a set of plastic drawers. She punched holes in the bottom and installed the wheels herself. This relatively small investment saves me days of scrubbing and hours of lining shelves, taking down boxes, unpacking and setting up my Pesach kitchen, as well as redoing all that after Pesach. Whoever I share this tip with thanks me profusely.

Making Pesach during a Crisis

Chani: I'll have to figure out which of these great ideas will work for me. The few times I made Pesach at home were when my family was going through a difficult period. Since I'm often on bed rest when I am expecting, and my pregnancies have coincided with Pesach, I've had to perfect my "crisis management" approach to Pesach.

Friends, relatives and cleaning help

The first thing I did was call all the local *chessed* organizations, my relatives, friends and neighbors. This was not the time to be bashful. I was pleasantly surprised to see how much people had to offer, some cleaning help, some babysitters, some meals, and some even offered money.

I gave a lot of thought to how to maximize all the help I was getting. I saved all the heavy duty jobs for the *bachurim* who do cleaning before Pesach — the oven, fridge, etc. I gave the cleaning ladies the tables, chairs, beds, laundry, floors and cabinets. My teenage babysitter did closet shelves and other odds and ends. I was constantly using my brain to think creatively. How can this twelve-year-old babysitter "kill two birds with one stone"? One time I sent her on a Pesach errand with the children. Another time, I had her clean the toys together with them.

When meals from neighbors and organizations didn't work out, we ate frozen foods and takeout. I taught several of my children how to use the sandwich maker and microwave.

Clarity in the laws of Pesach

With all that underway, it was still never enough help. I realized that I had to change my mindset and distinguish between *chumros* and *halachos*. I knew it would be incorrect to sacrifice my sanity or my *shalom bayis* for the sake of stringencies. My husband called our Rav for very clear guidelines on how to make a purely *halachic* Pesach. I was relieved to learn that there are many places in the home which do not have to be cleaned, especially if the *chametz* in them are sold. There are a number of clear and reader-friendly *sefarim* available which explain this, also. *Guidelines* by Rav Barclay and Rav Jaeger and Rav Sheinberg's sheets are just a sampling.

With clarity in *halachah*, a smile plastered on my face, and a closed eye to all that was flying around me, I made it to Pesach that year! I had a few dedicated neighbors and relatives who were happy to cook for us on Pesach. We filled in what was missing with "Pesach takeout." It was quite expensive, but I tried not to think about the price. It was necessary and well worth the money. Having enough food is crucial on Pesach. It is superfluous to mention, but I *davened* a lot for success in our preparations. With tremendous *siyata diShmaya*, a lowering of expectations and a lot of *chessed*, we made a happy and kosher Pesach!

Managing Your Family throughout Pesach Preps

Tova: I think some of your ideas should be implemented by all of us — not only by women in crisis — to achieve a happy and kosher Pesach!

A very large detail that has always baffled me when preparing for Pesach is, what is my family supposed to be doing while I am steeped in preparations? How much help can I expect of them? How can I maintain the usual serenity of my home throughout the tumultuous time of Pesach preparation? My ultimate goal, of course, is to create positive associations with Pesach preparations for my children. I've discussed this with many friends and, combining their ideas with my own, I came up with a way that this can be achieved.

It's so important to have realistic expectations. We can't just ignore our children, so we have two choices: either involve them in the cleaning or help them find entertainment.

Realistic expectations

In order to gain clarity, I categorized my family into different age brackets.

1. Youngest ages — babies to four years: I acknowledged that I couldn't expect to clean while they were around. I either needed a babysitter or a dedicated older child to take them out or to seriously occupy them. I thought about how to make this work, and made up my mind that it was worth a little financial investment, since I didn't want them to undo my efforts, but I also didn't want to be upset with them for just being children.

2. Middle ages — five to eight years old: These children can potentially be a real help. They can also entertain themselves nicely, if I would relate to them properly while I clean. So when they helped, I praised them a lot, played relaxing music in the background, kept my expectations low and hoped for the best. It is preferable to get less done and maintain the warmth in your home, to get more done, but at the expense of positive feelings. No sergeant barking for me! I scheduled all the heavy cleaning for when this age children are not around.

Pesach Activities for Ages 5–8

- Clean toys, kitchen set, doll carriages
- Be your extra hands — pass you things while you are standing on a step ladder
- Run errands within the house or to a close neighbor
- Empty drawers, check for pieces of *chametz* (*k'zayis*), and refill

- Pair lost socks
- Prepare a "camp" for younger children. Mommy provides prizes, treats and supplies.
- Clean with spray bottles filled with water and a little bit of soap
- Scrub chairs, walls, tiles, or grimy corners with a toothbrush
- Decorate house or Seder table with pictures and other Pesach paraphernalia

3. **Older children — nine and up:** These children can really make my work load lighter. I give them choices, and they pick which jobs they would like to do. We sit down with a snack and make a schedule together, deciding during which part of the day they will help and during which part they are free. By doing this, I avoid having to nag them throughout the day. It is crystal clear to my children what is expected of them, and they are willing to help, because they are the ones who choose their jobs and their schedule. When necessary, we work together.

I don't overload them with work. Just because I'm moving like a locomotive doesn't mean they have to. The ultimate responsibility of Pesach is on me, not on them.

Praise and rewards

I constantly give them specific praises, always letting them know how their efforts give me more time and energy to clean, to go shopping, to make lunch, to allow me to nap, etc. When I inspect their work, I give only compliments. If something isn't done properly, I quietly fix it myself later.

One year, I even did a point system for every job they did. The prize for helping was a day trip with Daddy or Bubby and Zeidy in the midst of all the cleaning. It's very normal for kids to get burnt out and not want to help for an entire day, even under the best of circumstances. I enjoy a quiet day of cleaning and they all come home with a new burst of energy to help me the next day.

Providing activities   I also invest in some quality arts and crafts supplies for both the older and younger children. I find it is worth my while to spend some money to keep our home *b'simchah* throughout Pesach preparations. It fosters such positive feelings that often my children start offering to help of their own free will.

Erev Pesach foods   **Sarah:** Sounds wonderful. I never thought about the long-term Pesach attitudes I am giving over to my children as I prepare. But Tova, how do you handle meals?

Tova: Thanks for reminding me! I find it extremely important to feed my family properly on *erev* Pesach. In fact, when my husband asked our Rav for advice on Pesach cleaning, the first thing he was told was, "Remember to eat!" Hungry husbands and children (and mothers) only exacerbate the *erev* Pesach pressure and promote negativity in the home.

Thanks to your suggestion, Sarah, last *erev* Pesach I had some well-balanced meals in my freezer; the only problem was that I ran out! Here is my greatest food tip for *erev* Pesach — frozen pita sandwiches. Pita makes significantly fewer crumbs than bread. A few weeks before Pesach, I bought over forty pitas and spent time filling them with cheese and ketchup, peanut butter and jelly, veggie burgers, baked beans, tuna — you name it! They were all wrapped carefully and put in the freezer. At meal time, when the kitchen was already off limits, I had my sandwich maker set up outside and I just popped in the ready-made sandwiches. The kids ate their favorite sandwiches with minimum crumbs and no preparations.

I must say, I only do this when I'm watching. Otherwise, I don't allow my kids to get their hands on *chametz* during Nisan. I give them many non-*chametz* snacks, like ice pops, fruits and vegetables, as well as *kitniyos*, like rice cakes, popcorn, and Bamba. I prefer to ban *chametz* inside the house, even a few weeks in advance, rather than to be on guard all day reminding my children to be more careful!

Also, as soon as I turn over, I don't cook for Yom Tov right away. The first thing I do is cook a nice meal for immediate consumption.

After sticking to these ideas for a number of years, I noticed a significant change in the attitudes of my family members. They greeted Yom Tov in good spirits and without any resentment. With a lot of thought and a little practice, it is possible to make Pesach and still be *b'simchah*.

No-fuss Food and Snacks for the Month of Nisan

- Kosher for Pesach deli and hotdogs
- Chicken and rice meals prepared in advance and frozen
- Pareve hot dogs
- Instant mashed potatoes
- Canned beans

- Potatoes and cheese in microwave
- Pasta (no crumbs)
- Rice cake sandwiches
- Pita sandwiches (use pita instead of *challah* on Shabbos HaGadol)
- Bagged salads
- Raw baby carrots
- Canned vegetables and fruits (pickles, corn, pineapple, etc.)
- Fresh vegetables and fruits
- Yogurts and puddings
- Ices
- Sugary treats (no crumbs)
- Bamba, chips and popcorn

Summer —
Sivan, Tamuz, Av

Chapter 13

Recharging

Making the Time

Tova: I just became a member at the local pool this season. I find it so invigorating and relaxing to go swimming. All my tension gets washed away. Would anyone like to join me? It would be fun to go with a friend!

Sarah: You are so incredibly busy. Where do you find the time?

Finding someone to take over **Tova:** I just make the time. I hire a babysitter, trade off with a neighbor, ask my parents to take over, or bribe an older child to help. The key is that I'm determined to recharge myself because I know how crucial it is to my mental health. Bottom line, my responsibilities don't run away while I'm swimming. They're still there waiting for me, and anyway, even if I don't take the time off, I'm never finished with the things I have to do — there's always something waiting to be taken care of. What do you do to recharge, Sarah?

Sarah: I enjoy walking, either with my husband or with a friend. When I walk with my husband, we leave our cell phones at home. It's refreshing to have a nice conversation outside the home without the telephone ringing, household chores staring at me and children interrupting us. When I walk with a friend, I enjoy the social time; if I don't make the effort, days can go by without speaking to a single friend.

Tova: See, you also find the time!

Sarah: It's true. But I'm working on getting rid of that guilty feeling when I walk out the door. There is always something important that I feel I should be doing instead of going for a walk.

Tova: Of course! At this stage of our lives, we are always busy with something important. Prioritizing for us doesn't necessarily mean choosing something more important over something less important, but taking care of an immediate need. When I choose to wash the dishes or prepare dinner, I'm automatically not doing something equally important like folding laundry or washing the sticky floor. Whatever we choose to do always comes at the expense of something else that needs to get done. Remember, all the members of our families draw their strength from us, so we have to maintain our own strength. You shouldn't feel any guilt over taking that time out to recharge yourself. Whatever else you needed to do will wait for you.

Taking care of needs

Sarah: I hear what you're saying. I agree. I should try to let go of the guilt. But I still don't get how you can commit to a membership at the swimming pool. Don't you find it to be such an ordeal to fit into your schedule?

Tova: Right now I feel up to the commitment. I'm excited about it. I never make a commitment for more than a few months at a time, since you never know what can come up. In this way, any activity that I take on does not become such a burden. I do always make sure that I'm doing some form of exercise, but I'm constantly reevaluating and changing what it is according to my needs and my family's needs.

No long-term commitments

Chani: I have the same attitude towards my weekly *shiur*. Right now it's easier for me to get out at night. Other times I have found it easier to go to a morning shiur. I always make sure that I go to some *shiur* at least once a week. I find it keeps me inspired and uplifts my entire week!

Reasons to Recharge

Dena: I have no time for any extras during my week. I don't know how much I really need it, though, since I feel that my work itself recharges me. Working out of the house also helps me appreciate the time that I have with my kids.

Recharging in order to give

Tova: That's so nice to hear! Unfortunately, there are many women today who don't get enough satisfaction out of caring for their families. Giving to our husbands and children ideally should be what charges us, not drains us. We are really part of a new generation, though, and most of us need to make sure to take time to restock our resources in order to give. Exercising, socializing, going to *shiurim* or pursuing a hobby — everyone has to do what works for her. If you're lucky and enjoy your job, you can recharge at work. Eating healthy and getting enough sleep is also a must.

I've trained myself to become a balanced giver — to take care of myself so that I can give a lot of myself. When I learned to do this properly, I became a much happier person and a better wife and mother.

How to Recharge

Dena: I would love to go around the room to hear everyone's little secrets about what they do to keep themselves energized. I probably would enjoy something other than work and could find small slots of time to stick something in; I just have to figure out what the right thing is. What else do you do besides swim, Tova?

Tova: I try to always have my finger on the pulse. I try to understand my nature, respect it and attend to it accordingly. For example, sometimes in the middle of a harried afternoon, I just go into my room for twenty minutes and read a magazine, even if it's not so convenient for everyone else. I tell the kids that I'm resting and I am! I decorated my room with fake plants, and I make sure it's always clean and pretty and a welcoming place to relax in. I treated myself to one of those massage contraptions at the Sharper Image and I use it for a quick relaxing fix. *Twenty-minute relaxation break*

Chani: I make sure to take the time to eat very healthy. I'm not stingy with my own meals. I make sure to be stocked with the foods that I like to eat, not just what the kids like. I make sure to eat lots of vegetables and whole grains. *Nutrition*

Vitamins, not coffee, are key for me. I find that women rarely have the energy they need for all the things they need to do, especially during their childbearing years. Vitamin B-complex and Omega3, which I take on a regular basis, keep me from feeling run down and tired. Taking these vitamins has changed the quality of my life entirely and I sincerely recommend them to all busy and tired women. I also take a multi-vitamin when I'm pregnant and nursing to make sure that my own body stays stocked with what it needs. Whenever I'm lazy and stop taking my vitamins, I really feel the difference.

I also often go on walks with my husband. I find that speaking outside the home adds quality to the time that we spend together.

Sometimes, when I feel like I need some pampering,

I treat myself to a nice warm bath with lavender oil. It's super relaxing.

Sarah: Speaking my thoughts out — with Hashem, with myself and with friends — has worked very nicely for me when I need to renew my strength. I speak all day with Hashem, constantly asking for help with every little detail. These little *tefillos* all day long are my main way of recharging. When the baby is screaming, the kids are fighting, the house is a mess and I can hardly get dinner from the freezer to the microwave, I try to ask myself, "What is the *ratzon* Hashem right now?" What would Hashem like me to handle first? This allows me to slowly and steadily deal with whatever situation is before me until everything is taken care of. Making proper decisions with Hashem in mind gets me through the day.

I also keep certain key phrases or quotes in my mind that I have collected from different role models over the years. "There are a million and one ways to be a good mother," (Rebbetzin Altusky) and "I can only put in the effort, but the success is in the hands of Hashem," and "I am only human." Tova, I've added your phrase to my list: "A home has to be clean enough to be healthy, but messy enough to be happy." The list goes on and on. Sometimes I write these quotes down and hang them up on the refrigerator as reminders. Talking to myself and being my own source of *chizuk* has worked very successfully for me.

I try not to get too caught up on how little sleep I got — I never count the hours. Lack of sleep does not have to mean that my day is doomed! I try to keep a positive mindset, no matter what, and that helps me through a lot of frustrating moments.

I make sure to have good conversations often with a friend on a walk or on the phone. I'll even put it on my list of things to do, because I know how important it is for my mental health. This resource group, besides giving me great ideas, does me a lot of good in this area. Half the time I come just for the social aspect. It's refreshing to hear how all of you deal with your own everyday issues and it gives me strength to deal with mine.

Speaking with friends

Dena: Come to think of it, I do have a few things I do to recharge. For one, I try very hard to find the time to *daven Minchah* as often as I can. It doesn't take me so long and I feel it is my special connection to Hashem during the day.

Davening Minchah

I also enjoy reading books. Somehow, I always manage to find the time. Also, every morning, I jump around my room and do the few exercises and stretches that I remember from classes that I once took. It helps me start the day on the right foot.

Reading, exercising and resting

I always try to make sure to nap on the days when I have time available. I could never keep up my busy schedule without those naps.

I would love to one day take sewing lessons to domesticate myself a little more, or pick up where I left off on my childhood piano lessons. I think both would be good for me. Maybe this summer I'll be able to create the time for something like that. You are all inspiring me.

Extra-curricular activity

Chapter 14

Family Vacation

Planning a Vacation

Chani: I need some vacation ideas. All my kids are at different stages and it's been a challenge to come up with a vacation that suits everyone's needs. I would love to make everyone happy!

Mommy's attitude

Tova: I have found that it doesn't really matter where we go or what we do; it's all in my attitude. It's nice just to get away as a family! Wherever we choose to go has the potential to be fun. The key for me is not to let the details of our trip overwhelm me. I try to stay relaxed, because I know that my state of mind affects everyone else's ability to enjoy our time together.

In the past when we have gone away in the summer, my husband learns in the morning with the boys. The girls sleep late, lounge around, play a little and get ready. In the afternoon, we'll do a family activity. Going to a nearby park is a lot of fun when Daddy comes along and plays with the kids. We come up with some creative ways to make even an ordinary park become more fun. What could be better than that!

Family bonding in the park

One of our favorite vacation activities is building a big homemade tent in a park. You just tie a rope around two trees and drop a sheet over it, securing it with clothespins at the top and rocks on the bottom. Then we sit in the tent to eat, play games and tell stories.

To make our time in a park a little different than usual, we time the kids to see how fast they can climb, swing, slide, and use all the park facilities. Then we time them doing all the same things while holding a cup of water, and challenge them to try not to spill! Freeze tag is always popular, and so is kite-flying, Frisbee, and games with balls. Even a new bottle of bubbles can go a long way. I see that my older girls who don't like playing in the park anymore, enjoy these family trips — it's a bonding experience for everyone in the family.

Sarah: Wow, that sounds very special. I wish it were so easy. Frankly, my kids don't enjoy each other's company and would never go for a bonding day in the park. We need real activities!

Whenever we go on vacation, I always have all the days' activities and details planned out in advance. I make sure that our itinerary contains activities that will interest kids of different ages and genders, so that by the end of our vacation, everyone feels that their vacation needs were tended to. Of course, my schedule never works out exactly as planned, but at least it gives us a framework from which to work. I don't want to get stuck in the middle of vacation spending half the day figuring out what there is to do, what we should do first and how to get there. Especially, when we go with other families or friends, it is worthwhile to have these time-consuming, planning conversations beforehand. *Planning in advance*

Chani: I don't even know how to begin to plan a vacation! Where would I start?

Sarah: The best place to start is to ask around where people have gone. I never go anywhere without a recommendation. You can also look in the local *frum* magazines for ideas. If you are traveling with little children and/or you don't have access to a car, it's best to pick a place where most of the activities are in the immediate area. If you have a car that fits everyone comfortably, then you have more options. Before we go, I make a master information *Information sheet*

sheet which includes men's and women's hours at the pool, local cab numbers, pizza and take-out numbers, addresses of *shuls* and times of *minyanim*, as well as the hours of other available activities, all costs and travel times. Finding out all this information in advance, allows our days to be fuller and more fun. If our plans don't work out one day, this information sheet allows me to come up with a backup plan almost immediately. I recommend not trying to cram too many activities into one day. We always try to get our money's worth out of each place we go. It's less exhausting that way and more enjoyable not having the pressure to rush to the next activity.

Tova: Knowing you, you probably also make a menu plan in advance.

Bringing along food

Sarah: Of course it's the easiest to go to a place that serves meals. Even then, I always bring bread, peanut butter and jelly, cheese and an electric sandwich maker for my fussy eaters. I also bring plenty of carbohydrate snacks for between meals, like crackers, rice cakes, and pretzels. I don't want my or any of the children having their day spoiled due to hunger.

If we're going to a place where I will be in charge of food preparation, I make a very unvaried, practical and easy menu. Healthy food is not my number one priority on these vacations. For lunch we'll have noodles, veggie burgers, tuna or other sandwiches, or — everyone's favorite — grilled cheese. Our sandwich maker works overtime on these special vacations. Dinner is deli, barbecue or pre-prepared meals from home. Frozen french fries and frozen pizza also make for a popular easy meal. For veggies, I bring canned pickles, corn, bagged salad or I cut up cucumber and carrot sticks. Knowing what we'll be eating and preparing it in advance allows me to also enjoy our family vacation. Coming prepared also avoids having to buy food at the vacation spot, where it is usually much more expensive and might not have the kosher certification that we need.

Chani: I think I'll tag along on your next vacation! You seem to really know what you're talking about.

Sarah: Well, after a few years of poorly planned vacations, *kvetchy*, hungry children, an overwhelmed Mommy and wasted money, I finally got my system down!

Tova: Do you really plan an activity for every hour of vacation?

Sarah: No, of course not. There is always a lot of down time. Even on the most exciting and well-planned vacation, there always seems to be time either between activities or in the early morning or late evening with nothing to do. I always bring a few new books that the kids haven't seen, some new travel games, old magazines and some interesting arts and crafts projects. It is in this area that I've noted the benefits of going away with other families. There is more fun, less complaining and less need for *shlepping* toys.

Down time

Dena, you go away a lot. Do you have anything to add?

Packing for a Trip

Dena: We usually go away for a week in the winter, either one month or two in the summer, plus numerous weekends throughout the year. It has its advantages and disadvantages, like everything else. Packing is difficult for a larger family — sometimes I think it's easier to stay home — but by now, I'm ready to patent my own special packing method for large families!

Making a packing list

First I make a packing list depending on where we are going. If I will have access to a washing machine, I cut the quantities of clothing in half and make sure to do laundry while we're away. Some people see it as a chore to do laundry, if they are only going a way for a week or two, but I love it because we take only half the amount of luggage and there is less unpacking and laundry to do when we get back. The older children pack their own belongings according to the list and I pack for the younger ones. I take extra clothing only for the children who I think will need it.

Using see-through bags

Unless we are going away for an entire summer, we don't usually unpack, even if it's for a week or two. I give each child their own clear, large-size zip-lock storage bag to pack in (or any other similar type bag, such as the kind that down blankets come packed in). I taught them to pack in separate piles so that all the various articles of clothing, like shirts, pants, skirts and undergarments are easily accessible at all times and they don't have to flip over one thing to get to the next. I can fit three of these bags in a duffle. When we arrive at our destination, we just put our clear plastic bags on top of the dresser or in a corner of the room. Everyone can see what they have and they just live out of their bag. This system reduces the risk of losing clothing and belongings, and also prevents clothing mix-ups between children.

Sarah: What a great idea to have a clear bag! I do something similar, but with carry-on bags. Each child gets their own carry-on or shopping bag with their name on it. We pack up each duffle with a few bags inside. The children can't always find what they need though, so sometimes they end up dumping everything out of their bags, which creates unnecessary messes. I think I'll try your suggestion next time.

Dena: We've also invested in strong luggage. All of our duffel bags have wheels and a pulley. If my husband pulls his back out by trying to carry our luggage, our whole vacation is ruined.

Children's small, personal traveling bag

Each of my children has a knapsack with them at all times. It makes my own personal bag smaller, and that way I don't have to tend to their every need at every moment. They each carry their own snacks, drink, gum, a travel game, book, crayons, a pad of paper, hat, "barf bag" and an extra shirt and underwear, if necessary. I have a child who gets very car sick, so he packs a change of clothing in his carry-on; that way we don't have to go searching through all the luggage. I always keep tissues, safety pins, band-aids and wet wipes in my bag, even when I don't have a baby with me; they're helpful in all sorts of situations.

I used to find that one of the most time-consuming packing jobs was the toiletry bag. Rethinking what we needed each time and rummaging around the bathroom cabinets looking for small bottles for shampoo and for half empty toothpaste tubes took more time and energy than necessary. I finally decided to invest in a spare, permanent toiletry bag with all the toiletries, creams and

Packing toiletries

even antibiotics that we would ever need while away. I found a good assortment of miniature travel toiletries in the drugstore and I stocked up on some. When the bottles are finished, I refill them from our stock in the house. I don't ever unpack this toiletry bag so it's easy to just add it to the suitcase.

Sarah: Now I'm looking forward to our next vacation just so I can put all these packing tips into action!

Packing Lists
[Items in the spare toiletry bag]

- ☑ Advil — adult and child
- ☑ Anti-bacterial cream
- ☑ Antibiotics
- ☑ Antihistamine
- ☑ Band-aids
- ☑ Brush
- ☑ Calamine lotion
- ☑ Conditioner
- ☑ Cover-up
- ☑ Extra vitamins
- ☑ Gauze pads and tape
- ☑ Hand lotion
- ☑ Hand sanitizers
- ☑ Insurance information
- ☑ Iodine
- ☑ Lipstick
- ☑ Personal hygiene items
- ☑ Safety pins
- ☑ Shampoo
- ☑ Soap
- ☑ Spare glasses, if necessary
- ☑ Spray deodorant
- ☑ Suntan lotion
- ☑ Travel sewing kit
- ☑ Travel toothbrushes
- ☑ Tylenol — adult and child
- ☑ Various medications, as needed
- ☑ Wet wipes

It sounds like a lot, but fits very nicely into a regular size toiletry bag.

[Stuff to bring]

☑ Alarm clock

☑ Baby toys

☑ Beach toys

☑ Bicycles/outdoor toys, if necessary

☑ Blow-up toys for the pool

☑ Books

☑ Cell phones and chargers

☑ Clothing for all the days plus one extra per person

☑ Extra socks

☑ Hair accessories

☑ Hats

☑ Juice cups

☑ Pacifiers

☑ Robes

☑ Sandwich maker

☑ Slippers

☑ Snacks, snacks and more snacks

☑ Travel games

☑ T-shirts for the pool

☑ Undergarments

☑ Water bottles and holders

Chapter 15
Prioritizing

Time Management

Tova: Dena, how do you manage to do it all? You keep a clean and organized home, serve well-balanced meals, satisfy all of your family's needs, take care of yourself and you even work! You are so confident and competent in all areas! What is your secret?

Chani: Please don't tell me. I don't need any more things to work on.

Clarifying goals

Dena: It's not a secret at all. I'm happy to share; I just don't know if what works for me will work for anyone else. Basically, I have clarity about what my priorities are throughout my day. Since my days are so packed, I have had to become very focused on what I need to be doing at each point in my day; otherwise I won't fit it all in.

For example, I don't take any phone calls at all in the middle of bedtime, because that's my special bonding time with the children. I don't clean up when I'm supposed to be preparing lunch; I just close my eyes to the mess. I don't organize an entire bedroom as I'm putting away laundry. Most importantly, I don't let myself feel guilty when I can't get to something since I decided to tend to something more important for the moment.

Chani: I don't think I ever could have such an intense schedule, being so disciplined with my time like that. I'm much more laid-back. I don't milk every moment to its capacity. My family benefits from this because I've created a relaxed, warm and happy atmosphere in the home. On the other hand, I don't get to a lot of things, and my husband and children feel it. It bothers me so much.

I always feel guilty over whatever I'm not getting to.

If I did a beautiful job straightening up, I feel guilty that *Guilt over* I didn't have enough time to cook a proper dinner. If I *things not tended to* cooked a special meal, I'll feel bad that I didn't give certain children enough attention that day. Every once in a while, my mother-in-law will call at the absolute worst hour and then I'll feel guilty that I haven't taken the time to speak to her lately. I feel negligent when I don't make time for myself and I feel spoiled when I take too much time for myself.

Everything I do is always at the expense of something else! How can I fit everything into my life and not feel guilty over what I didn't tend to?

Dena: This is exactly my point. You need clarity. You *Committing* need to learn how to prioritize within your day and feel *to a decision* comfortable with the activities you chose to do that day. Once you've given it thought and committed to a decision, you'll feel comfortable with yourself as you confront all the things you haven't tended to.

Chani: It's just not my style to account for every moment of my day. I'm not a machine like you, Dena.

Dena: But you do want to rid yourself of guilt and become more productive. Listen, I'll teach you the formula that I use for prioritizing. It's worth hearing me out even if it's not your style of thinking, and giving it a try will help you to get clear on your own priorities.

Tova: I can't even imagine a guilt-free day!

Sarah: You have certainly piqued my interest. Although I do get a lot done, there are always those equally important things that I have dropped that I feel bad about.

Listing life categories

Dena: Okay, let's get started. I learned to prioritize properly from Julie Morgenstern's excellent book, *Time Management from the Inside Out*.

First, I clarified my goals in all the different categories of my life. I wrote down all the important various life categories, such as, marriage, parenting, extended family responsibilities, *chessed* outside the home, self-development/*ruchnius*, self-care, home maintenance and extra-curricular activities. These are all the categories that I wanted to fit into my life somehow. Just writing it all down already helped me focus.

Then I wrote down pointed questions for each category, and pushed myself to answer them. Here are some examples:

What are my goals in marriage?

What are my goals for my children?

What are my financial goals? Do I work too much? Too little?

What kind of relationship would I like to have with my mother-in-law and sister-in-law?

How can I include proper *davening* habits into my schedule?

How much exercise and extra-curricular activities do I need to keep me going?

Understanding yourself

Tova: I get so caught up in the business of life that I often forget what I'm striving for. What a wonderful idea to reevaluate your goals in such a systematic way!

Dena: There's a catch. After clarifying my priorities and setting my goals, I had to make sure that they were within reach. They had to suit my personality and be realistic within my own personal strengths and weaknesses.

For example, as a working mother, it's unlikely that I will be able to devote much time to community work because then I won't have sufficient time to spend with my family. If I am an expecting, working mother, then I have to allot more time for resting and cut out something else that would otherwise be a priority.

For better or for worse, a messy home makes me crazy, although I prefer to work rather than to clean all day. I hire cleaning help to pick up my slack. I often buy salads for Shabbos so that I can benefit from my husband's free time Thursday evenings and go out for a walk with him. Chopping vegetables is so time-consuming!

Looking at the big picture of my life in a snapshot view helps me address all my life goals, weighing and balancing each one against the other as needed. Doing this gives me the strength to feel confident about my choices and not feel guilty about saying No when I have to.

Tova: Tell me if I'm getting this right. You're saying that I can't reach the goal of having a spotless home if I hate cleaning and I don't hire help.

Working with who you are

Dena: Exactly. That's the kind of goal that will have you constantly feeling guilty. You have to work with who you are. Set a realistic goal, keeping in mind how much time you think you can handle cleaning and straightening up.

Tova: So, if I really would like my home to be spotless, then maybe I should consider bringing in more help. It will free up my time to do things that I enjoy more, like creative cooking and spending time with my children.

Chani: Do you mean to say that if I hate cleaning, folding laundry, washing dishes and making sandwiches, I can just skip it without feeling guilty, because it doesn't work with my personality?

Being creative to reach goals

Dena: Let's not exaggerate. I also don't love doing all the jobs that I do, yet I still have to do them. However, you can be creative with the kind of help you hire or the jobs you delegate. If you really despise folding laundry, you might hire an older, capable child to fold all your laundry and put it away once a week. I used to hire a sixteen-year-old to wash my dishes, wipe down the counters and clean up the toys for an hour every evening. It's much cheaper than hiring a proper cleaning lady and it made a big difference in the functioning of my home. Maybe you can teach one of your children to prepare the sandwiches. "Think out of the box," as Tova always says.

Chani: I probably would find more time to cook if my counters and sinks looked more inviting. Cooking healthy food for my family is important to me. Maybe it is worthwhile to ask my neighbor's older daughter if she's interested in some light housework a few nights a week.

Rewarding yourself

Dena: Now you're getting the idea. Everything does have to get done, but you have to work with your strengths and weaknesses. Not against them. If you don't want to hire help and you need a push to do it yourself, pay yourself or buy yourself small presents, once a week, as a reward.

Chani: Maybe I'll buy myself a new plant that I had my eye on — guilt free!

Sarah: I think my yoga instructor would understand what you're saying. She told me that I should drop yoga and switch to aerobics. All those relaxing stretches were just boring me. She said that she could tell that I needed to jump around more. I have so many friends who enjoy yoga, so I wanted to make it work for me, but it only frustrated me.

Chani: I love yoga. It really gives me a charge!

Sarah: That figures. This is exactly Dena's point. How about with a newborn? That's always a hard time for me. According to you, Dena, should I lower my cleanliness standards because my priority then is nursing my baby?

Dena: Actually, I would say just the opposite. If you feel you need to hire more help at that time, so hire it. You seem to crave cleanliness and orderliness for your sanity. Recognize that this is both your strength and your weakness. With a needy newborn around, it is sometimes impossible to keep to even minimum standards of cleanliness. Any free time a new mother has is usually dedicated to basic meal preparation, laundry and resting. Of course you should lower your expectations, but only to a point that you can function. Don't try to be a hero. If I were you, I would definitely hire more help after having a baby.

Strengths and weaknesses

Tova: I'm getting the hang of this idea, but honestly, I'm not really clear on what my preferences, strengths and weaknesses are.

Dena: I came up with a list of questions based on Julie Morgenstern's book that you can ask yourself. They helped me to understand myself better. Answering them truthfully also helped me with the final step in the prioritizing process — creating my own personal weekly and monthly schedule. Knowing what works for me allows me to really tailor-make a realistic schedule for myself.

Self-Analysis Questions

(Based on *Time Management from the Inside Out*
by Julie Morgenstern)

I. What I'm Successful At:

1. I always make time to ——————— no matter how full my schedule is.

2. I don't waste time on ———————.

3. I am clear about the following goals:

   ———————.

4. I don't procrastinate when it comes to:

   ———————.

5. I'm always on time for ———————.

6. I can find time to exercise when

   ———————.

7. I have no problem saying No to ———————.

8. I am very happy when I ———————.

9. I have no problem delegating the following jobs:

   ———————.

10. I'm able to make time for myself when

    ———————.

II. What Is Challenging for Me:

1. It's hard for me to find the time to

   ———————.

2. I waste too much time on ———————.

3. I am unclear about the following goals:

   ———————.

4. I wish I could find time to ——————— every day.

5. I never properly estimate the amount of time it takes to _____.

6. I always push off this activity, responsibility or chore: _____.

7. I'm usually late for _____.

8. I usually say Yes to _____ even though I shouldn't.

9. It's hard for me to focus on _____.

10. It's hard for me to make decisions about

_____.

III. Personal Preferences

I enjoy :

- Working alone/Working together with others
- Exercising by myself/Exercising in a group
- Focusing on one thing at a time/Multitasking
- An action-packed schedule/A slow, laid-back schedule
- Scheduled plans/Spontaneous plans
- Quiet/Music or other noise
- Working under pressure/Spacing tasks
- Keeping things simple/Making things fancy
- Socializing/Keeping to myself

IV. Time Preferences

It works well for me to accomplish _____ in the mornings.

It works well for me to accomplish _____ in the afternoons.

It works well for me to accomplish _____ in the evenings.

It works well for me to accomplish _____ late at night.

Mornings are a bad time for _____.

Afternoons are a bad time for _____.

Evenings are a bad time for _____.

Late night is a bad time for _____.

The beginning of the week is a better time to

_____.

The end of the week is a better time to _____.

Erev Shabbos is a bad time for _____.

Motza'ei Shabbos is a good time for _____.

Creating a time map

Dena: After I did all my homework, I was equipped to create a practical schedule for myself. I drew up four big maps of the week, breaking each day into 3 slots of time, morning, afternoon and evening. I proceeded to play a sophisticated form of Sudoku, fitting in all the necessary activities to accomplish all of my goals.

Home maintenance goals

I'll give you a few examples of how to fill out this time map. In my life category of home maintenance, my goals are to:

1. Have a clean and organized home.
2. Be able to provide healthy meals and clean clothing for my family.

The specific activities I came up with to accomplish this are:

1. Cook and freeze.

2. Create a workable laundry schedule.

3. Allot time to straighten up on a daily basis.

4. Hire cleaning help for deeper cleaning.

5. Make time for projects that are building up.

On my time map:

1. I scheduled "cook and freeze" for my day off every other week.

2. I start the wash every morning before I go to work and then dry, fold and put away when I return home from work.

3. The family straightens up every evening immediately after dinner. I came up with a "chore" system.

4. My cleaning help comes on Wednesday.

5. One Sunday a month, I take care of errands that are building up, such as, taking the mending pile to the seamstress, taking the new serving dishes to the *mikveh* or taking the *sheimos* to the *genizah*.

Here's another example. In my category of extended family, my goals are to:

Extended family goals

1. Maintain a close relationship without interfering with my work or family schedules and routines.

2. Really be concerned for them and know how they are doing.

The specific activities I came up with are:

1. To call my mother and mother-in-law every morning from my cell phone on the way to work.

2. To call a different sister or sister-in-law every day on my way home from work.

3. I make sure to give some thought to their lives
first so that I am able to ask them specific questions about how they're doing.

Other goals   My specific activities for my goals in marriage, parenting and work appear in my schedule every day in some
form or another. Self-care also shows up every day in the
kinds of food that I eat and quick morning exercises that I
do. Self-development and *ruchnius* appear on my time map
usually once or twice a week in the form of a *shiur* or a call
to *Chazak* hot-line. Every day, I make sure to schedule in a
time for *Minchah*.

Tova: Come on! You mean to say that you make a
monthly schedule for yourself and then stick to it the entire month?!

Monthly   **Dena:** Of course, my schedule doesn't work out exactly
schedule   as I planned. Changes and additions are constantly com-
with weekly
revisions   ing up. I make a vague time map by the month, planning
four weeks at a time, and then every *motza'ei* Shabbos I sit
down and revise it to fit the upcoming week.

My month's calendar contains my work schedule,
cooking schedule, a slot for a big shopping, cleaning days,
shiurim, appointments, morning and evening routines,
straightening up schedules and allotted time to help with
homework and study for tests.

In my weekly revisions, I add in important phone
calls, errands and other needs that have come up for that
week. I make changes all the time in my schedule. Since I
am working off a basic calendar, all my life categories are
addressed and my important goals don't get lost. In any
given week, even big things have to go as I am prioritizing. Sometimes, if I'm especially exhausted, I might even

dare to cancel my child's therapy appointment so that I could take a nap, if I feel it's crucial to the functioning of my family.

When you begin using this method, it might take a few months of revisions until you find a schedule that fits your needs and goals. Of course with every added child or other changes in your life, you have to readjust your time map again according to the new needs.

Tova: You sound so focused! No wonder you accomplish *Daily lists* so much, Dena. I'm not as thorough as you with my prioritizing but I consider myself pretty responsible with managing my time properly. I work with lists. I make a daily "must-do" list on my fridge and then a separate running list of what I would like to accomplish during the week. Every night, I sit down and make a new list for the next day. Keeping these lists works well for me as long as I don't let myself feel guilty over what I haven't accomplished. Often, though, I feel bad at the end of the day when I transfer half my list to the next day's list. I really should make sure that I only write down what is truly feasible for that day on my daily list.

My weekly list is broken down into time segments. For example: a list of things that I can do in five minutes or less, such as scheduling an appointment, throwing in a simple wash, sewing on a button or saying Tehillim for someone. Then I have my half-an-hour or less list — mix together a quick cake for a birthday party, clean out one messy drawer or shelf, vacuum the bedrooms, fold one load of laundry, etc. Sometimes I'll find an unplanned small stretch of time where all the children are playing nicely or got invited out to friends. I don't waste time thinking about how to maximize the time. I quickly estimate how much time I think I have, refer to my list and accomplish.

Sarah: None of these ideas seem too hard. I just have to set aside some time to work on them. It would be so nice to get rid of my perpetual pangs of guilt.

Chani: What's a Jewish mother without pangs of guilt? It's part of our biological makeup!

No-guilt approach   **Dena:**   It's counterproductive! I feel that if I have done my best to responsibly plan out my time, keeping in mind the needs of my family, home and self, then there is no reason for me to feel any guilt. What more can I expect of myself? I'm a human being. There will always be some equally important mitzvah or chore that I could have been doing. My responsibility as a wife, mother and homemaker is to work with the strengths and weaknesses Hashem has given me and to serve Him in the best way possible. If that's what I'm striving for and working on, then guilt is superfluous. Guilt just hinders my productivity and masks my progress.

Chani: Thanks, Dena. You've definitely given us a new and more positive way to look at things.

Afterword

Start Your Own Resource Group

You Can Do It, Too

(as appeared in *Mishpacha Magazine*,
May 2008, by Bassi Gruen)

Interested in starting your own resource group? Go for it! Here are some pointers to help you get started:

- **Pick brains and build up a core group** — It's important to make sure that you have a few enthusiastic supporters of your idea before you begin working out the details. Speak to these women about how they'd like the group to run, how often, where, at what times they'd like to meet and what topics interest them. Ideally, a meeting should be at least one hour long. It should not meet more often than every other week, as it takes time to absorb and implement new ideas.

- **Have a strong facilitator** — If you want your meetings to be as productive as possible, you need a facilitator willing to keep an eye on the clock and making sure that every participant has a chance to talk.

- **Keep it homogenous.** When the group consists of women who are in the same stage of life, it will have a good chance of running smoothly. Our group consisted of women who were married for ten to fifteen years and mothers to four to eight children, and we found that we were all on the same page and had the same concerns. A newlywed could never understand our obsession with laundry ("What's the problem? Just throw in two loads each Wednesday!"), while a woman with married children would be restless listening to our discussions about the Shabbos table ("You think bored toddlers are trouble — just wait until you have to host your future daughter-in-law!").

- **For lively dynamics, it's best to have ten to twelve women at each session,** although smaller could work as well. In order to have this number at each meeting, you will need a commitment from a much larger group, probably around twenty women. With dentist appointments, sick kids, and other emergencies, you need to assume that at least one third of the women won't be able to come to each individual session, but if you have a big pool of women, you'll have enough participants each week.

- **Watch for pitfalls.** From the outset, it should be clear that the group is meant to be purely productive. Do not let it degenerate into a *kvetch* clutch. Any *lashon ha-ra* or gripes about children and spouses should be avoided. In addition, the members should exercise sensitivity. Raving about a husband's dishwashing prowess, or mentioning faithful Maria who comes two hours each morning, may sting those who don't have such assistance.

- **A reminder call the night before is essential** — particularly if the group does not meet weekly. You can arrange a chain call so that none of the women gets saddled with all the calls.

- **Be flexible** — Take this basic template and fine-tune it to fit the interests of your group. The possibilities are endless. You can run the group once a month and have each woman bring a dish for a potluck supper. You can add on fun activities, like games or quizzes, if you want to stress the social aspect of the meeting over the practical features. If you want your group to have a more professional flavor, you can occasionally invite outside experts, women famed for their organizational prowess or cake decorating skills. Do what works best for you.

I'm interested in hearing how YOU manage. Do you have great techniques or tips that work for your personality? Please share your ideas with me and I'll pass them along to women who can use the advice. Be in touch at YaelWiesner@gmail.com.